Uniforms of Waterloo

Easy ys myne boke to rede and telleth of moche fyte
But then your easy rede is damned hard to wryte
(Napier)

Philip J. Haythornthwaite

Uniforms of Waterloo
16–18 June 1815

Illustration by *Jack Cassin-Scott* and *Michael Chappell*

ARMS AND
ARMOUR

First published in 1974 by Blandford Press

This edition published by
Arms and Armour Press
An imprint of the Cassell Group
Cassell plc, Wellington House,
125 Strand, London WC2R 0BB

Distributed in the United States by Sterling Publishing
Co., Inc., 387 Park Avenue South,
New York, NY 10016–8810

British Library Cataloguing-in-Publication Data
A catalogue entry for this title is available from the
British Library

ISBN 1–85409–394–0

Printed in Hong Kong by
Dah Hua Printing Press Co.

CONTENTS

AUTHOR'S NOTE

This book was first published in 1974 as part of the Blandford Press Colour Series, and in subsequent editions thereafter. In the present edition, the plates and text are reproduced unchanged, but the opportunity has been taken to provide an expanded bibliography, listing additional important works, and including some of the relevant material which has appeared in print since the publication of the original edition.

INTRODUCTION

The Waterloo Campaign of 1815 has become the most famous of the nineteenth century. It is of interest for three reasons: first, it was of short duration, and fought over a very small area, thus making study in depth comparatively easy; secondly, it marked the end of twenty-five years' warfare, and proved the final overthrow of Napoleon Bonaparte; and thirdly, because of its far-reaching consequences, it prompted the production of a larger number of books than any other campaign, both histories and personal reminiscences.

This book is concerned with one aspect of the campaign: the uniforms of the opposing armies. Unlike other works which include the subject, this does not try to show what the troops should have worn according to their own regulations, but what they *actually* wore, whether versions of full dress, modified for the rigours of campaigning, specially-designed 'campaign dress', or in some cases completely non-regulation costume. To cover the subject completely in eighty plates is well-nigh an impossibility, but together with the text to the plates, the uniform of every corps engaged in the three days of fighting is described, and every branch of every army illustrated.

It is difficult to say with any certainty exactly what uniforms were worn by any particular regiment between 16 and 18 June 1815. With few exceptions, the costume of the British and Netherlands armies presents few problems, but the French troops, chronically short of equipment, were in some cases dressed in a myriad of unusual and non-regulation styles: it has been reported that even some regiments of the Imperial Guard did not contain twenty men in identical attire. The question is further complicated by the predominant habit of officers of wearing non-regulation items of uniform, occasionally of their own design; and sometimes whole regiments were dressed contrary to regulations: the British 16th Light Dragoons, for example, wore jackets officially superseded in 1812, while some of the Nassauers still clung to the uniform of their days in the Confederation of the Rhine.

There is insufficient space for any highly detailed account of the campaign, but a short history of the climactic events of June 1815 has been included, together with two maps which illustrate basic troop movements between 16 and 18 June. Some regimental details have been noted as part of the text to the plates, and the actions of any unit can be determined by reference to the Appendix on the 'Orders of Battle' of the three opposing armies.

The unit strengths given should be regarded as approximate, because complements naturally varied from day to day. All statistics, including casualty figures, are taken from Siborne, except in those cases where official returns are specifically quoted. No casualty figures are available for some regiments, and the losses sustained by the French Army can only be guessed.

In some cases sources disagree on minor details of brigade and divisional organisation; the 'Orders of Battle' given in the Appendix are in all probability those in use on 18 June 1815, though it is possible that some units may have been detached from their parent formations; the exact brigading of the French Imperial Guard still remains unknown. In a few instances, the 'Orders of Battle' differ from those given by Siborne, these changes being the result of detailed research. For those wishing to compare these lists with Siborne's, it should be noted that in a few cases Prussian units are listed in the latter work by their 'provincial' number (i.e. 1st Silesian) rather than their number in the line.

Finally, it is inevitable that some information on the uniforms has, for lack of space, been omitted in illustrated form; some uniforms varied greatly even within the same regiment. In addition, there are probably some details which have even yet not come to light. However, the uniforms illustrated are, in all probability, those actually worn by the combatants in Europe's most decisive battle of the age.

THE WATERLOO CAMPAIGN

(Note: for details of troop movements during the campaign, reference should be made to the two maps.)

After twenty-five years of war, peace came to Europe in 1814 when Napoleon Bonaparte, Emperor of the French and one-time master of the largest European empire since Rome, abdicated his throne. Exiled to Elba to brood over his misfortunes, Europe returned to a state akin to that before the French Revolution, with the Bourbon monarchy, in the person of the obese Louis XVIII, restored to its rightful place. The statesmen of Europe travelled to Vienna to distribute the spoils made available by the defeat of France; with them went the Duke of Wellington, victor of the Peninsular War which had been a major factor in Napoleon's defeat. Their peace was rudely shattered by the news that Napoleon had disembarked a force of some 1,200 men in southern France on 1 March 1815 and was advancing on Paris.

The superficial loyalty to Louis XVIII evaporated instantly as both people and troops flocked around the standards of their ex-Emperor; the King himself fled. The Allied nations responsible for his defeat once again pledged to overthrow Bonaparte, and a plan was produced whereby British, Prussian, Austrian and Russian armies would advance on Paris. Napoleon's one ally, Murat, King of Naples, took the field in support of the Emperor, but was crushed before he could receive any French aid.

Napoleon, by recalling all undischarged troops and mobilising the National Guard to relieve front-line units, assembled an army of something in excess of 124,000 men, many poorly-equipped, with which he hoped to march on Brussels, defeating the first Allied armies before the others could attack, and then, in a position of considerable strength, sue for peace on his own terms, or continue to fight as necessary. By the end of the summer he hoped to have about 600,000 men capable of taking the field.

To oppose Napoleon's advance on the Netherlands, two of the Allied armies were assembling. The first was basically Anglo-Dutch, commanded by the Duke of Wellington, with the young and incompetent Prince of Orange nominally second-in-command; he commanded the whole until Wellington's arrival from Vienna. The Prince's appointment was political, as was that of the eighteen-year-old Prince Frederick of the Netherlands, who was given command of a Division.

The core of the Anglo-Allied army was the British contingent, which contained some Peninsular veterans, but also many 'young' battalions and half-trained recruits. In addition, there were some battalions of the magnificent King's German Legion, a 'foreign corps' composed basically of Hanoverians. The other Hanoverian troops in Wellington's army were both regulars and militia battalions of mixed quality, though (with one notable exception) they acquitted themselves with credit. The Netherlands detachment was a different matter; many of the Belgian troops had fought under Napoleon, and loyalties were mixed; though some of the units were to fight bravely, the Netherlands troops were of doubtful quality, and suffered heavily from desertion. The presence of the inexperienced Prince of Orange did not improve matters. The Duke of Brunswick's 'corps', though containing some veterans, was largely composed of recruits, who, while performing well on occasion, could not be depended upon. The Nassau contingent was one of the better parts of the army. Wellington organised the units under his command so that recruits and units of dubious quality were brigaded with seasoned troops, in such a way that no brigade or division would be untrustworthy, each containing some dependable troops; it also helped to prevent mass desertion. The Duke had some justification for calling it 'an infamous army'. Its strength gradually increased until on the eve of the campaign it numbered about 92,000.

The second Allied army, to work in conjunction with Wellington, was Prussian, under the command of the active septuagenarian, Field-Marshal Blücher. Though one of his own staff described him as quite incapable of understanding a plan of campaign, old Blücher compensated for it by his bravery and determination, born of a deep-rooted hatred for the French. To assist him, his capable Chief of Staff, Gneisenau, practically ran the Prussian army, though for reasons best known to himself, Gneisenau mistrusted Wellington. Blücher's army at the beginning of hostilities numbered about 120,000, including a considerable number of militia or 'Landwehr'. Together, the two Allied armies were to prove more than a match for Napoleon, though, in Wellington's words, it was a 'close-run thing'.

The Battle of Ligny

The Allied armies were based on Brussels and Namur, but, unexpectedly, it was Napoleon who attacked first, crossing the frontier on 15 June, and engaging the Prussian skirmishers almost at once. However, Allied movements showed no haste; Wellington even attended the Duchess of Richmond's ball in Brussels that night, in order not to panic the citizens by appearing preoccupied with the French attack; many of the Anglo-Dutch staff also attended the ball, giving Wellington a good opportunity to issue his orders. When the ball finally broke up, it was because a message arrived to say Napoleon had occupied Charleroi. Wellington set his army in motion immediately, so quickly that some of the British officers had no time to change from their ball dress.

Napoleon planned to attack one of the Allied armies before the other could link up; he chose to fall upon Wellington first, then turn upon Blücher. However, to do this he had to drive back the Prussian troops beyond Gembloux. Napoleon therefore detached Marshal Ney with some 24,000 to hold back the Anglo-Dutch army which was gathering at Quatre Bras, while he dealt with the Prussians; he intended Ney to assist him if the Anglo-Dutch forces retired. The attack on the Prussians commenced at about 3 p.m. on 16 June at the villages around Ligny; Napoleon intended to drive in the Prussian centre, with Ney hopefully coming up to envelop Blücher's right wing, and administer the *coup de grâce*. But things did not

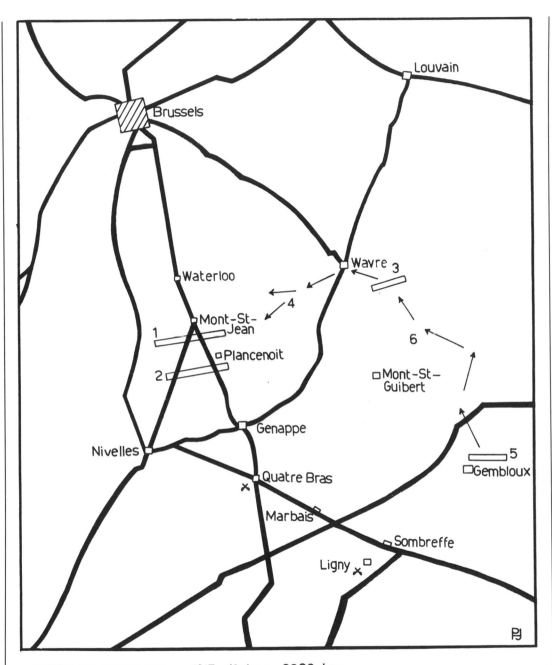

WATERLOO CAMPAIGN — 1815. 18 June 0900 hrs.

1. Wellington   4. Prussian advance to Mont—St—Jean
2. Napoleon   5. Grouchy
3. Blücher   6. French advance on Wavre
✗ — actions of 16 June

Fig 1.

go as planned. After hours of bitter hand-to-hand fighting around the villages, with the fortunes of battle swinging back and forth, Napoleon decided to launch his main attack even though Ney – now heavily engaged himself – could not possibly come to his assistance. To make matters worse, D'Erlon's French corps was occupied in marching between Ney and Napoleon, both screaming for reinforcements, with the result that poor D'Erlon reinforced neither, not knowing where he was most wanted.

When Napoleon launched his main assault on the Prussian positions, however, Blücher's centre, after a heroic resistance, collapsed, and it appeared as if the entire Prussian army might be destroyed. In pouring rain, the French stormed Ligny; only two brigades of Prussian cavalry were available to stem the French tide, and these were led by the gallant old Blücher himself. In the ensuing mêlée, Blücher's horse was killed and fell upon him, and the battle continued around him. Dragged from beneath his horse, the Prussian commander was borne away semi-conscious. Though the Prussian centre was destroyed and in flight, the wings retired in good order and the French did not pursue. Gneisenau, temporarily in command, gave orders to withdraw to Wavre. Napoleon had won a considerable victory, with the loss of some 12,000 men; the Prussians had lost about 16,000, and another 8,000 deserted during the night.

The Battle of Quatre Bras

Meanwhile, Ney had attacked the Prince of Orange at Quatre Bras; Wellington arrived at about 3 p.m. to find many of the Netherlands units already retiring in disorder, though Prince Bernhard of Saxe-Weimar's Nassauers were fighting gallantly. Elements of Wellington's army were arriving throughout the action, but less than half were present even at the close. At first, Wellington's position was desperate; he had a few British troops (from Picton's Division), the Duke of Brunswick's corps, the Nassauers and the unsteady Netherlanders; his only cavalry, the 6th Prussian Hussars, had rejoined their own army. Ordering his British infantry to advance on the French, which they did with conspicuous success, Wellington sent the Brunswick infantry to assist the gallant Nassauers who were still fighting grimly but losing heavily. The Duke of Brunswick charged with his Hussars, but retired without seriously damaging the French; while rallying his men, the Duke was mortally wounded.

The Prince of Orange, hearing of Brunswick's death, brought up Van

Merlen's Netherlands cavalry brigade to support the Brunswick Hussars and Lancers, and led the whole formation towards the French. Confronted by a brigade of French cavalry, the Netherlands cavalry fled in disorder before contact had been made, the outnumbered Brunswickers being forced to retire with them. Wellington himself tried to rally the cavalry just south of Quatre Bras, but was almost surrounded by French and only escaped by leaping his horse over the 92nd Highlanders, deployed in line, who drove the French cavalry back. Two British battalions – the 42nd Highlanders and 44th Foot – were caught before they could form a square, the universal defence against cavalry; the 42nd closed their square with a large number of French cavalry *inside*, and killed them all; the 44th made no attempt to form a square, their rear rank turning round, and the battalion fighting back-to-back, decimated the attacking French. Some of the Netherlands cavalry reformed and returned to the action. At last the Nassauers were being pushed back, but were still hanging on.

Ney launched a Cuirassier attack, which was driven off by the 92nd, 42nd and 44th; Best's Hanoverian Brigade and the Brunswick cavalry completed the rout of the French. All this time, the Allied infantry was suffering severely from French artillery fire. More reinforcements arrived just in time to save Wellington's left flank from being overrun; Wellington himself directed their movements, leaving the centre temporarily under Sir Thomas Picton's control. Picton was reinforced by Colin Halkett's brigade of four British battalions; these he formed in square as a protection against the French cavalry. The Prince of Orange, however, resenting Picton's interference, ordered all four battalions into line, suicidal tactics if French cavlry were in the area. They were; the 69th Foot was ridden down and ceased to exist as an operational unit for the day, losing a Colour to the 8th Cuirassiers. The 33rd and 73rd Foot behaved poorly, breaking before the French hit them; they fled into Bossu wood with some casualties. Only the 30th Foot formed square and retired in good order; the Prince of Orange had made his first of three ghastly mistakes. Wellington rallied three of the smashed battalions, but the position was desperate. The arrival of Cook's British Guards Division and more artillery stabilised the line.

Wellington then took the initiative and ordered a general attack; the 92nd stormed a French strongpoint with fixed bayonets, and along the whole line the French were thrown back. Ney broke off the action with perhaps 4,500 casualties; the Allies lost slightly more, including 2,275 British; however, many of the Allied 'losses' were the result of Netherlands deserters being returned as 'missing'.

Withdrawal to Waterloo

On the following day, 17 June, both Allied armies withdrew, the Prussians to Wavre, and Wellington to a small hamlet on the Brussels road, Mont-Sainte-Jean, on a ridge just south of the village of Waterloo. This position had been mapped on the Duke's instruction in 1814, and on 15 June he told the Duke of Richmond that the ridge was the place he intended to engage Napoleon, provided he could be sure of the assistance of at least one Prussian corps. Napoleon, having rejoined Ney with the bulk of his army, some 72,000, detached Marshal Grouchy with 33,000 men to follow and harass the Prussians; Grouchy, however, was not informed how vital it was for Napoleon that the Prussians should be prevented from linking up with Wellington. A set of unfortunate circumstances were to result in Grouchy playing little part in the events of 18 June; his corps could have ensured a French victory had it been present at Mont-Sainte-Jean.

The Prussian plan was to consolidate around Wavre, then move at least some elements of their army towards Wellington; old Blücher, back in command after his fall, was determined to support the Anglo-Netherlands force, though Gneisenau apparently had doubts about Wellington's integrity, suspecting that he might withdraw and leave the Prussians alone. But Blücher was adamant; he would link up with Wellington on the 18th. As it happened, the Prussian movement was greatly delayed in setting off and progress slowed down by the churned-up mudpits which masqueraded as roads.

Wellington withdrew to his position at Mont-Sainte-Jean with a minimum of difficulty, though there was some skirmishing with the French cavalry. The position he had chosen for his stand was a good one: the line was based upon the Ohain–Braine l'Alleud road, which in parts was slightly sunken, with a bank at either side. The ridge had a slight 'reverse slope', so much a feature of Wellington's Peninsular victories, behind which troops could shelter, immune from enemy fire. At the rear of the position was a wooded area which would have provided shelter if the army were forced to retreat. Hedges of considerable size protected part of the British front, and the position was made stronger by the possession of three fortified points, the château, farm and woods of Hougoumont, the farm of La Haie Sainte, and the villages of Papelotte, La Haye and Frischermont. It was a good defensive position, but the right flank could have been exposed; to combat this threat Wellington detached a force of about 15,500 men at Tubize and Hal, some eight miles west of Hougoumont. The

Duke has been much criticised for this action, as those troops were not engaged at any time; but there were sound reasons for his actions. The position at Mont-Sainte-Jean was made safe from being outflanked, and the troops sent to Hal contained only one British and one Hanoverian brigade, the remainder being of doubtful quality; it also removed Prince Frederick from the danger area.

Wellington garrisoned Hougoumont with the light companies of the British Guards Division, together with some Hanoverians and Nassauers; the position was reinforced throughout the day by Cooke's Guards who occupied the road north of the château. Chassé's Netherlands Division was placed farther west, in Braine l'Alleud; it was brought closer in later in the day. Wellington's reserve, the Brunswick corps and Clinton's Division, was posted near Merbe-Braine, where they could stop any French attack west of Hougoumont. Between Cooke's Guards and the Genappe road was Alten's reliable Anglo-Hanoverian Division, and on the east of the road was Picton's Division, with Bylandt's Netherlanders drawn up slightly in front. The Papelotte–La Haie position was held by Nassauers. The farm of La Haie Sainte was held by the 2nd Light Battalion of the King's German Legion under Major Baring, supported by a detachment of the 95th Rifles in a sandpit north of the farm enclosure. The cavalry was drawn up behind the front line.

Both armies spent a wretched night, the French coming up all the time. Thunderstorms and drenching rain, no shelter, and a shortage of rations on both sides dampened the spirits of all but the most seasoned campaigners. The early hours of 18 June were spent in cleaning weapons, checking ammunition, and Hougoumont, La Haie Sainte and Papelotte were fortified, a barricade going up on the Genappe road just south of La Haie Sainte. Napoleon had almost 74,000 men drawn up before the Anglo-Allied position, numerically outnumbering Wellington, and when quality was considered the odds would have been overwhelmingly on the French, had it not been for Blücher's promised assistance.

Hougoumont

At about 11.50 a.m. on 18 June, the battle began with an attack on Hougoumont. Jerome's Division poured into the Hougoumont woods, but the Hanoverian and Nassau sharpshooters retired before them in good order, maintaining a most destructive fire. Coming out of the woods the French walked into a murderous fusillade from the British Guards in the fortified buildings, and recoiled in disorder. As they retreated, Wellington himself directed the fire of a howitzer battery which swept the French with shrapnel and shell-fire; not a Frenchman was left alive in the Hougoumont enclosure, and the woods were recovered.

The attack was soon renewed, this time with the assistance of part of Foy's Division, striking both east and south sides of the position. A counter-attack by four companies from the 2nd Guards on the ridge cleared the French from the east wall, but a party of French outflanked the position and stormed the northern gate. Lieutenant Legros of the 1st Light Infantry smashed in the gate with a pioneer's axe, and the French stormed into the courtyard; after a desperate fight Colonel James Macdonnell, in command at Hougoumont, personally closed the gate and the position was saved, but it had been a 'near-run thing'. Hougoumont was reinforced by more British Guards, the garrison now numbering about 600. Again the woods were taken; soon all of Byng's Guards Brigade, save for two companies, was in the buildings, plus the 2nd Line Battalion of the German Legion, and eventually the Brunswick Avant-Garde, with the line north of the château suitably reinforced from Wellington's reserve. For about ninety minutes the only serious action on the whole field was around Hougoumont, and when the engagement became general, the fight continued; the woods and orchard were taken and retaken, but no Frenchman got inside the buildings, even when they were set ablaze by French howitzer fire. Large numbers of French troops were expended without achieving any useful purpose; Wellington used only about 3,500 men to hold the position, who kept over 14,000 French occupied throughout the day. As many as 10,000 fell in the fight for the position, three-quarters of them French.

The first attack

Napoleon now assembled a battery of eighty guns on a ridge east of the Genappe road, which began to fire on the Allied position. Bylandt's Netherlanders, in an exposed position, broke and fled. The first French attack began; the divisions of Allix, Marcognet, Durutte and Donzelot, with some of Bachelu's, advanced, driving the Allied skirmishers before them. The Allied artillery opened on the advancing troops, who were now attacking the Germans in La Haie Sainte. Realising the danger of sending reinforcements to Major Baring's men in the farm, Wellington left them exposed; the Prince of Orange, however, ordered the Lüneburg Battalion to counter-attack the French infantry, moving them forward in line; as with the 69th at Quatre Bras, they were overrun by Cuirassiers and destroyed.

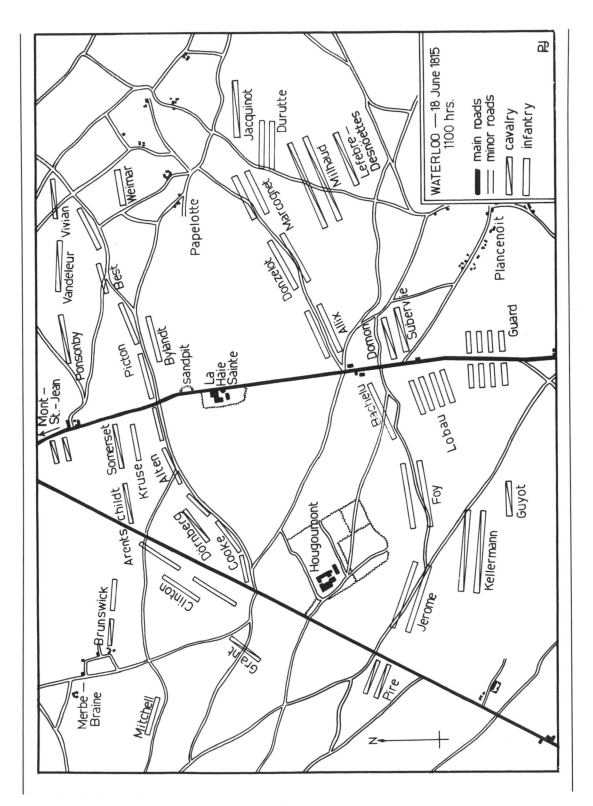

Fig 2.

The French infantry was torn by Allied artillery fire; obeying orders, prior to being overrun, the Allied artillerymen abandoned their cannon and retired to the cover of the infantry. The French advance was partially halted by British musketry, but Allix's men still came on, supported by the Cuirassiers; but the French horsemen were swept back by a charge of the British Household Cavalry. Then Ponsonby's 'Union' Brigade of the British 1st, 2nd and 6th Dragoons was launched at the French infantry. Donzelot's entire division was completely smashed, and the British attack spread into Marcognet's; at the same time, Somerset's Household Cavalry hit Allix's infantry. The carnage was horrific; with the exception of Durutte's Division, the French attacking force temporarily ceased to exist; two 'Eagle' standards were captured, along with over 3,000 prisoners.

Triumph now turned to tragedy for the Allies; the cavalry charged on, cutting through the eighty-gun battery and beyond; all control was lost, and the disorganised British heavy cavalry was all but destroyed when counter-attacked by French cavalry on fresh horses. Sir William Ponsonby, commander of the 'Union' Brigade, was killed. Their retreat was covered by Vivian and Vandeleur's British and German Legion's light cavalry and by rockets fired from Whinyates' Battery of the Rocket Corps. The French attack had been beaten off, but at the cost of half the effective Allied cavalry, and Sir Thomas Picton, who had been shot through the head.

The French cavalry attacks

Bylandt's Brigade had reformed in part, but was incapable of returning to the front line; the troops around Merbe-Braine were moved in towards the centre. Another French infantry attack threatened La Haie Sainte, but the German Legion defenders held on; the place was set afire, but a battalion of Nassauers arrived in time to use their cooking-pots as fire-buckets, and the danger subsided. The French artillery opened up again, preluding an attack by cavalry. An incredible attack: the first charge was made by 5,000 horsemen on a front of only 700 yards, allowing no space for manoeuvre. The Allied infantry formed into squares, commencing rolling volleys of musketry. The result was never in doubt; the French were shot down in hundreds, but came on with fanatical courage. They were counter-charged by the British and German light cavalry alone (the Netherlanders refusing to move, and the Duke of Cumberland's Hanoverian Hussars leaving the field *en masse* and arriving in Brussels with the news that Napoleon had won), but that was enough; they were driven back down the slope, the Allied gunners running from the cover of the squares to fire their cannon into the backs of the retreating French. Wellington brought up Chassé's Netherlanders from Braine l'Alleud to reinforce his centre.

Ney attacked with his cavalry again, and continued to do so until over 10,000 men were engaged at any one time; the result was always the same. The French cavalry were first swept with canister and grape-shot from the Allied guns, then musketry, and cannon-fire again as they retired. One British battery, Mercer's of the Royal Horse Artillery, remained in action the whole time, building a ghastly wall of bodies in front of their position as the French were cut down in scores. Mercer compared the French cavalry to grass being scythed down by a mower.

At 4.30 p.m. Wellington heard a cannonade from the south-east, indicating that some Prussians were in action, though not as yet actively supporting him. The final French cavalry attack came at about 5.30 p.m., delivered at a walk because of the exhausted condition of the horses. It was the heaviest attack, and suffered the heaviest slaughter; the whole line gave way, and did not return. The finest cavalry in Europe had been destroyed by tactics which even now cannot be fully explained. Another attack, combining infantry, cavalry and artillery, hit the Allied line behind Hougoumont; it was driven off with the loss of some of the cannon, abandoned near the Allied line.

The Prussian arrival

The Prussians, given that their movement to support Wellington would begin at about 7 a.m., should have covered the eight miles from Wavre, even over appalling roads, by 2 p.m. at the latest; their delay was caused partly by a fire in Wavre which partially blocked the road, and perhaps partly by Gneisenau's unexplained and ridiculous mistrust of Wellington. Even when they reached the area of combat, they attacked the French right rather than supporting Wellington directly. Between 4.30 and 5 p.m., Bülow's Corps, leading the Prussian army, attacked the village of Plancenoit on the French right flank, capturing the village. Napoleon counter-attacked with the Young Guard, throwing the Prussians back for more than a mile. Reinforced by Pirch's Corps, Bülow again took the village, but lost it again when elements of the Old Guard rallied the Young and cleared the area.

Everyone, Napoleon included, was now wondering what had become of Grouchy's 33,000 men. Ordered to follow the Prussians, Grouchy did just that, instead of marching to Mont-Sainte-Jean as Napoleon hoped. It was all he could do; to try and reinforce the Emperor might have resulted in a D'Erlon-like situation of 16 June, with Grouchy fulfilling no useful purpose. To contain his attack, Blücher detached Thielemann's Corps at Wavre, which, though outnumbered, kept Grouchy occupied while Blücher marched to support Wellington, in spite of Gneisenau's protests; to Blücher's stubborn determination to fulfil his promise to support the Anglo-Netherlands force must go much of the credit for Napoleon's defeat.

On Wellington's left, around the buildings of Papelotte, La Haie and Frischermont, the very first fighting of the day had occurred, though no serious losses were sustained. Prior to the destruction of the first infantry attack by the British cavalry, Durutte's Division had assaulted the area, but, in heavy fighting, Saxe-Weimar's Nassauers had held the position. The next attack on the Papelotte–La Haie area came at about 6 p.m. to 6.45 p.m., when Durutte again tried to take the buildings, again unsuccessfully; but then, just after 7 p.m., Zieten's Prussians came up to give Wellington his first real support. They mistook the Nassauers for French, and Saxe-Weimar thought he was being attacked by Grouchy. Tragically, the two Allied contingents engaged each other, the gallant Nassau troops inflicting heavy casualties on the Prussians before being driven from their barricades by sheer weight of numbers. The mistake realised, the Nassauers returned to their defensive positions, but were so exhausted that they could take no further part in the battle. They had held for ten hours and to them alone goes the credit for the defence of Wellington's left.

The fall of La Haie Sainte

With Lobau's Corps fully employed in holding the Prussians on his right, Napoleon's time was running out: he had to break the Anglo-Netherlands line quickly, or be defeated. Consequently, he ordered the capture of La Haie Sainte at all costs. Baring's original 376 defenders had been reinforced by elements of the 2nd Light and 5th Line Battalions of the King's German Legion, and by the Nassau detachment, but casualties had been heavy, and ammunition was running low. A massive French attack surged around the very walls, Frenchmen seizing the Legion's rifles as they protruded through the loopholes. The situation deteriorated, and then Baring ran out of ammunition. The French smashed down a door, and a desperate hand-to-hand fight began in the farmyard. Seeing the situation, the Prince of Orange decided to lend a hand. Still not having learned his lesson, he formed the 5th and 8th Line Battalions of the King's German Legion into line and advanced in support of the farm. They were caught by a body of French cavalry; the 5th managed to form square and retire under cover of a charge by the remnants of the British Household Cavalry, but the 8th were ridden down and destroyed. For the third time in as many days, the young prince had sacrificed a battalion to no purpose. Baring, at last, was forced to retire with his surviving forty-two men, all the remainder having gone down in the butt-and-bayonet fight in the yard. The remnants retreated to the sandpit, still held by the 95th, who then retired to the main position. The French now attacked the centre of the Allied line.

Wellington moved the 3rd Battalion of the 1st Guards forward to enfilade the French attack, forming square when threatened by a body of French cavalry. Adam's British brigade drove off the French infantry, who would have been massacred if the Netherlands cavalry had charged, but they still refused to move. In front of Alten's Division, however, things were not going so well, the Allied line being subjected to close-range artillery fire; the British 27th Foot was all but wiped out where it stood, while the 30th and 73rd were so depleted that they had to combine to form a square, as had the 33rd and the remnants of the 69th. Brigade commander Colin Halkett asked for a few moments' relief to reform, but Wellington told him that 'every Englishman on the field must die on the spot we now occupy'. Alten was wounded, and his division swept by fire; Kruse's Nassauers were in the same desperate position.

Then Wellington moved in his reserves; the Brunswick infantry came under fire and broke, but was rallied by Wellington himself; Vivian's cavalry formed in support. For a moment the issue hung in the balance, but the French were pushed back, leaving some of their artillery in Allied hands. The Prince of Orange had meanwhile ordered Kruse's Nassauers into line, but they broke and retreated before they could be overrun by cavalry, the usual effect of the Prince's orders. The young Prince, quite fearless in action, was at the forefront of the Allied position when he was knocked from his horse by a musket-ball, and carried from the field, wounded. As Prussian support came up on the left, Vandeleur's cavalry brigade was freed to strengthen the centre.

Napoleon's position was now desperate. Lobau's entire corps was needed to hold the Prussians, and still the Allied line remained intact, though Wellington's force had shrunk to perhaps 35,000, many Netherlanders having stolen away to positions of safety. Some of the Brunswickers were only held together by the presence nearby of Mercer's battery of horse artillery, while Colin Halkett's brigade was so depleted as to have been unfit for any further action, had not the situation demanded their presence in the front line. The cavalry of Vivian and Vandeleur, formed in line behind the front, prevented any mass desertion by the more questionable elements of Wellington's force.

Introduction

The final assault

Napoleon now gambled his last reserve, the infantry of the Imperial Guard, which had never once been vanquished. Accordingly, he sent forward two attacks against the Allied line, supported by all those troops who were available. Seven Guard battalions came up to the part of the line occupied by Maitland's British Guards, where Wellington himself was positioned. The Guards were lying prone until Wellington personally ordered them to stand up and fire at the French, now scarcely 40 yards away. As they fired at the Imperial Guard, the 52nd Light Infantry wheeled to enfilade their left flank, and the 33rd and 69th their right. The French, in column, could not reply effectively; hundreds died where they stood before the remainder broke and fled. At the same moment, the smaller Imperial Guard column had struck the Allied line and had driven back the 30th and 73rd Foot, together with the Brunswickers and Nassauers, but for once the Netherlanders, Chassé's Division, did a good job, holding the French until Wellington himself came up, rallied the Brunswick troops, and counterattacked. Fire from Krahmer's Netherlands artillery battery did the rest, and the second Imperial Guard column retired, leaving half its strength dead on the ridge.

That was the end. An incredulous cry of 'La Garde Recule' echoed along the French line, and the entire army began to disintegrate. Wellington ordered a general advance of the whole line, shouting to Colonel Colborne of the 52nd, 'Go on, go on! They won't stand. Don't give them a chance to rally'. Vivian and Vandeleur's light cavalry charged and the French retreat became a rout as panic set in. Only some battalions of the Grenadiers of the Imperial Guard, so far unengaged, stood their ground. The 2nd Battalion of the 3rd Grenadiers died where they stood. The 1st Grenadiers and a battery of Guard artillery continued to fire, but the remainder of Napoleon's force was a confused, fleeing mass. As Bülow's infantry emerged from the blazing Plancenoit, finally having defeated the French Guard units holding it, they broke into Luther's hymn 'A mighty Fortress is our God'; the last French units left the field, the 1st Grenadiers still in good order.

To the accompaniment of British cheers and a Prussian band playing 'God Save the King', Wellington and Blücher met near the inn of La Belle Alliance on the Genappe road. It was agreed that the Prussians, supervised by Gneisenau, should pursue and harrass the fugitive French; except for Vivian and Vandeleur's brigades, no Anglo-Netherlands unit was in any state to move. Whole battalions collapsed where they were from exhaustion regardless of the scenes of carnage around them.

As Napoleon's star finally slipped below the horizon, the moon rose over the most appalling scene of the entire Napoleonic Wars. In figures, the Anglo-Allied force had lost 15,000, the Prussians 7,000, and the French between 25,000 and 30,000. As one officer was to remark, it was usual after a battle to go to neighbouring units and ask 'Who's dead?', but in this case they asked 'Who's alive?' . . . the ditches around Hougoumont were choked with bodies, and huge piles of corpses marked the area where the French cavalry had been cut down, and one could see the position of the 27th's square by the dead, still lying in that formation. Worse than that was the condition of the wounded, many of whom lay three days before being treated. Parties of Belgian scavengers toured the field, murdering and robbing the wounded; looters from both Allied armies scoured the area, stripping the dead and living alike. Over the whole field arose a continuous moan . . . those who saw it acknowledged that the most sickening sight of all was in the Hougoumont enclosure, where a barn had been set alight, burning to death the scores of wounded, both French and British, who had been placed there. No person who witnessed the climactic events of the 16, 17 and 18 June 1815 can have doubted the truth of Wellington's statement that nothing but a battle lost can be half so melancholy as a battle won with such casualties.

The rest is easy to relate; although Grouchy had escaped in good order, Napoleon's main army was smashed beyond repair, and although sporadic fighting continued into September, the reign of Napoleon was effectively over by 10 p.m. of 18 June. The Battle of Waterloo, named from the village in which Wellington's headquarters were established, was one of the most decisive actions in the history of warfare. There is much truth in Wellington's remark, 'By God, I don't think it would have done if I had not been there.'

1   a) Duke of Wellington
    b) Major Henry Percy, ADC

2 a) Officer, Royal Horse Guards
  b) Trooper, 1st Life Guards

Britain

3   a) Trooper, 6th (Inniskilling) Dragoons
    b) Officer, 1st (King's) Dragoon Guards

4   a) Officer, 2nd (Royal North British) Dragoons
    b) Sergeant, 2nd (Royal North British) Dragoons

5 a) Trooper, 7th (Queen's Own), Hussars
   b) Officer, 10th (Prince of Wales's Own Royal) Hussars

6   a) Officer, 18th Hussars
    b) Trooper, 15th (King's) Hussars

Britain

7 a) Officer, 11th Light Dragoons
   b) Trooper, 12th (Prince of Wales's) Light Dragoons

8/9 a) Officer, Ro
   b) Gunner, Rc
   c) Gunner, M
   d) Officer, Ro
   e) Private, Co

Britain

10   a) Officer, 16th (Queen's) Light Dragoons
      b) N.C.O., 23rd Light Dragoons

Britain

11 a) Officer, Battalion Company, 1st Foot Guards
    b) Sergeant, Light Company, 2nd (Coldstream) Foot Guards

12　a) Sergeant, Light Company, 27th (Inniskilling) Regiment
　　b) Officer, Battalion Company, 4th (King's Own) Regiment

Britain

13 a) Private, Battalion Company, 28th (North Gloucestershire)
      Regiment
    b) Sergeant, Grenadier Company, 32nd (Cornwall) Regiment

14 a) Private, Grenadier Company, 73th (Highland) Regiment
    b) Officer, Light Company, 33rd (1st Yorkshire West Riding)
       Regiment

15   a) Officer, 51st (2nd Yorkshire West Riding) Light Infantry
     b) Private, 52nd (Oxfordshire) Light Infantry

16   a) Sergeant, 71st (Glasgow Highland) Light Infantry
      b) Field Officer, 42nd (Royal Highland) Regiment (Black Watch)

Britain

17 a) Sergeant, Battalion Company, 79th (Cameron) Highlanders
    b) Private, Grenadier Company, 92nd (Gordon) Highlanders

18 a) Rifleman, 95th Rifles
   b) Officer, 95th Rifles

19 a) Officer, Royal Waggon Train
    b) Officer, Royal Engineers

20   a) Officer, 2nd Light Dragoons, King's German Legion
     b) Trooper, 1st Light Dragoons, King's German Legion

21 a) Trooper, 3rd Hussars, King's German Legion
    b) Officer, 1st Hussars, King's German Legion

22 a) Officer, Battalion Company, 5th Line Battalion,
       King's German Legion
    b) Private, Grenadier Company, 8th Line Battalion
       King's German Legion

23 a) Officer, 2nd Light Battalion, King's German Legion
    b) Private, 1st Light Battalion, King's German Legion

Hanover

Hanover

26   a) Officer, Bremen and Verden Hussars
     b) Trooper, Duke of Cumberland's Hussars

Hanover

27   a) Officer, Landwehr
       b) Private, Landwehr

28 a) Officer, Foot Artillery
    b) Private, Foot Artillery

Brunswick

29 a) Officer, Lancer Squadron
     b) Trooper, Hussar Squadron

Brunswick

30 a) Private, Leib-Battalion
    b) Private, Avante-Garde Battalion

Brunswick

31   a) Officer, 1st Line Battalion
     b) Sergeant, 3rd Light Battalion

32   a) Duke of Brunswick
     b) Officer, Foot Artillery

Netherlands

33   a) Staff Officer
     b) Prince of Orange

34 a) Trumpeter, 2nd (Belgian) Carabiniers
b) Trooper, 1st (Dutch) Carabiniers

35   a) Gunner, Foot Artillery
     b) Officer, Horse Artillery

36 a) Flanquer, Dutch Infantry
b) Officer, Dutch Infantry

37 a) Grenadier Corporal, Belgian Infantry
    b) Officer, Belgian Infantry

38 a) Officer, Centre Company, 16th Jägers
    b) Hornist, Flanquer Company, 36th Jägers

39 a) Officer, 5th National Militia
    b) Private 1st Class, 19th National Militia

40/41   a) Trooper, 4th (Dutch) Light Dragoons
        b) Officer, 5th (Belgian) Light Dragoons
        c) Trooper, 6th (Dutch) Hussars
        d) Officer, 8th (Belgian) Hussars
        d) N.C.O., Guides te Paard

Netherlands

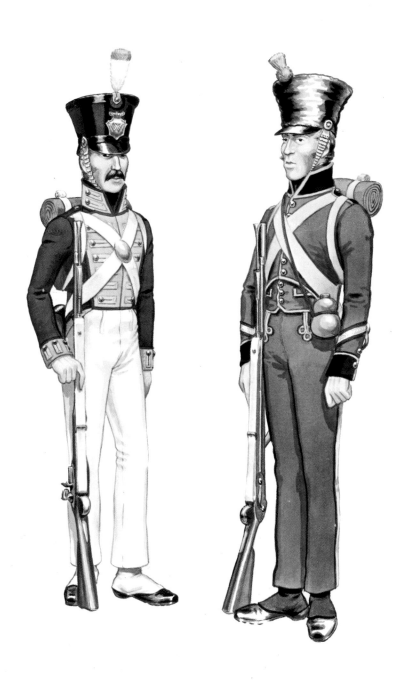

42   a) Private, Netherlands Indian Brigade
     b) Sergeant, 2nd Nassau Regiment

43 a) Flanquer, 1st Nassau Regiment
     b) Officer, 1st Nassau Regiment

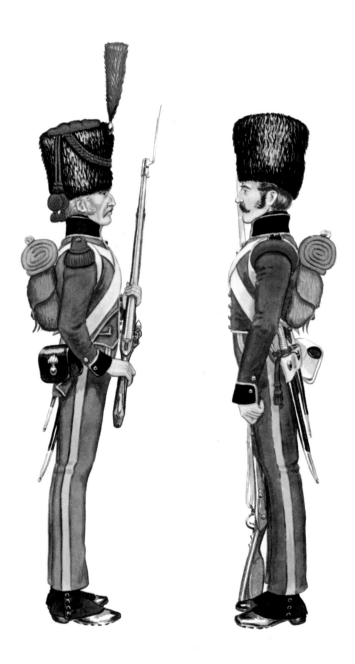

44   a) Grenadier, 2nd Nassau Regiment
     b) Grenadier, 1st Nassau Regiment

45   Napoleon

46 a) Trooper, Horse Grenadiers of the Imperial Guard
b) Officer, Dragoons of the Imperial Guard

France

47 a) Officer, Polish Squadron, Imperial Guard Lancer Regiment
    b) Trooper, 'Red' Squadron, Imperial Guard Lancer Regiment

48 a) Officer, Chasseurs à Cheval of the Imperial Guard
b) Trooper, Elite Gendarmes of the Imperial Guard

France

49 a) Private, Grenadiers of the Imperial Guard
      b) Officer, Grenadiers of the Imperial Guard

50 a) Chasseur, Chasseurs à Pied of the Imperial Guard
b) Sergeant, Chasseurs à Pied of the Imperial Guard

51 a) Officer, Voltigeurs of the Imperial Guard
    b) Private, Tirailleurs of the Imperial Guard

52 a) Officer, Horse Artillery of the Imperial Guard
    b) Gunner, Foot Artillery of the Imperial Guard

France

53 a) Private, Marines of the Imperial Guard
    b) Officer, Engineers of the Imperial Guard

54   a) Officer, 1st Cuirassiers
       b) Trooper, 11th Cuirassiers

France

55 a) Trooper, 2nd Dragoons
b) Officer, 7th Dragoons

56/57 a) Trooper, Elite C[...]
b) Officer, 6h Chev[...]
c) Brigadier, Elite C[...]
d) Trooper, 6th Ch[...]
e) Officer, Elite Co[...]

France

58   a) Officer, 1st Carabiniers
     b) Trooper, 2nd Carabiniers

France

59   a) Trooper, Elite Company, 1st Hussars
      b) Officer, 4th Hussars

60   a) Officer, Foot Artillery
        b) Private, Horse Artillery

France

61   a) Grenadier Officer, Line Infantry
       b) Eagle-Bearer, 45th Regiment

62   a) Fusilier, 1st Regiment
       b) Grenadier Sergeant, 72nd Regiment

France

63　a) Voltigeur Officer, Light Infantry
　　b) Voltigeur, 1st Light Infantry

64 a) Fusilier, 2nd Swiss Regiment
      b) Grenadier Officer, 2nd Swiss Regiment

Prussia

65   a) Adjutant-Offizier
     b) Generalfeldmarschal Blücher

66 a) Trooper, 1st 'Koningin' Dragoons
b) Officer, 2nd (1st West Prussian) Dragoons

Prussia

67   a) Officer, 4th (1st Silesian) Hussars
      b) Trooper, 6th (2nd Silesian) Hussars

68   a) Trumpeter, 3rd (Brandenburg) Hussars
b) Trooper, 9th (Rhenish) Hussars

Prussia

69 a) Fusilier Officer, 2nd (1st Pommeranian) Regiment
     b) Musketeer, 7th (2nd West Prussian) Regiment

70   a) Private, 1st Battalion, 12th Regiment
     b) Private, 25th Regiment

Prussia

71   a) Private, 1st Battalion, 21st Regiment
      b) Private, 3rd Battalion, 21st Regiment

Prussia

72/73   a) Officer, 1st U
           b) Trooper, 6th
           c) Trooper, 7th
           d) Trooper, 6th
           e) Trooper, 7th

Prussia

ex-Lützow's Friekorps)
ex-Hellwig's Streifkorps)
ex-Bremen Volunteers)
ex-Von Schill's Hussars)

74　a) Private, 2nd Battalion, 18th Regiment
　　b) Private, 31st Regiment

Prussia

75 a) Officer, Silesian 'Schützen' Battalion
b) Private, Volunteer Jäger Company, 7th Regiment

76 a) Officer, Westphalian Landwehr Cavalry
b) Trooper, Elbe Landwehr Cavalry

Prussia

77 a) Trooper, Neumark Landwehr Cavalry
b) Trooper, 3rd Silesian Landwehr Cavalry

78   a) Private, 1st Pommeranian Landwehr
     b) Officer, 1st Elbe Landwehr

Prussia

79   a) Gunner, Foot Artillery
     b) N.C.O., Horse Artillery

80   a) Driver, Train
     b) Krankenträger (Stretcher-bearer)

1. The Duke of Wellington. Major Henry Percy

Field-Marshal the Duke of Wellington, victor of the Peninsular War and commander of the Anglo-Allied army, is shown in this plate in the uniform he wore at Waterloo, his own design of semi-civilian dress. The low cocked hat bore cockades, of Britain, Portugal, Spain and Prussia; however, the hat was usually covered in a black oilskin 'waterproof'. The Duke's dark blue 'surtout' coat was covered by a cloak and cape of the same colour; a white neckcloth completed his dress. Note the absence of gloves, to which the Duke had a marked aversion! The sword carried by the Duke was, in fact, French, being made by the Imperial goldsmith, Biennais of Paris; how it came into Wellington's possession is not known, though probably it was a trophy of the Peninsular War. The large telescope was also carried at Waterloo.

The aide-de-camp shown with the Duke is Major Henry Percy, one of Wellington's eight A.D.C.s. Though an officer in the 14th Light Dragoons, he wore the staff uniform at Waterloo, minus the aigulette which was reserved for full dress. Percy is carrying a purple velvet handkerchief sachet, which provided one of the more romantic stories of the battle. When the Duchess of Richmond's ball was interrupted and Percy called away, the sachet was given to him by an unknown lady as a keepsake. On the night of the battle, Wellington wrote his famous 'Waterloo Despatch' announcing his victory, and entrusted Percy with the duty of conveying it to London. The document was placed in the sachet, and only removed when Percy, exhausted and still in his battle-stained uniform, presented the Despatch to the Prince Regent.

It was not unusual for British staff officers to wear civilian dress; for example, Lord Hill wore an old boat-cloak at Waterloo, and General Picton habitually wore a shabby greatcoat and a battered beaver hat, and arrived at the field of Waterloo carrying a green-lined white umbrella!

Casualties among the staff were heavy; in all, sixteen were killed, and thirty-nine wounded, and ten generals became casualties.

2. Great Britain: Officer, Royal Horse Guards. Trooper, 1st Life Guards

All three regiments of Household Cavalry were present at Waterloo, the two regiments of Life Guards and the Royal Horse Guards. The uniform of both corps of Life Guards was almost identical; all three wore the helmet with coloured woollen crest introduced in 1814. The Royal Horse Guards officer is shown in the laced full dress coatee, though at least one officer at Waterloo (Sir Robert Hill) wore a dark blue, single-breasted, buttoned jacket of the Life Guards style. The front of the Life Guards jacket (not shown in the illustration) was a simple, single-breasted version with brass buttons. Troopers were armed, in common with the remainder of the British heavy cavalry, with the 1796 pattern sabre, though officers of the Household Cavalry carried a unique pattern of sword, with gilt half-basket hilt. Sabretaches were carried by all ranks, though only officers used the ornate, laced version.

As part of Lord Somerset's Brigade, the Household Cavalry were heavily engaged in the battle, suffering casualties of fifteen officers and 305 men out of 696. Lt.-Col. Ferrior of the 1st Life Guards led no less than eleven charges before he fell, covered in wounds. At one stage in the action, Sir Robert Hill found himself surrounded by five French cuirassiers; he was rescued by Trooper Tom Evans of his regiment, who killed four of the Frenchmen before his sword broke, which compelled him to strike down the fifth with the broken hilt. Another notable incident concerned Captain Edward Kelly of the 2nd Life Guards, who, after killing an officer of the 1st Cuirassiers, calmly dismounted amid the heat of battle and cut off his victim's epaulettes as a trophy!

In the ranks of the same regiment was a noted pugilist, the giant John Shaw, one of the highest-ranked prize-fighters in England. After killing nine enemies in his regiment's first charge, Shaw was surrounded by ten Frenchmen. He accounted for five before his sword broke; flinging the hilt at one, he tore off his helmet to use as a club before he

was cut down. Struggling to rise, Shaw was shot, and crawled away to bleed to death on a dunghill during the night. He became a noted folk-hero of his native country.

3. Great Britain: Trooper, 6th (Inniskilling) Dragoons. Officer, 1st (King's) Dragoon Guards

The British heavy cavalry wore uniforms of a similar basic pattern, with regimental distinctions. The uniform was that introduced in 1812, the service dress including overalls with leather strapping. The plate on the front of the French-style helmet included a small oval plaque bearing the regimental title. Of the four heavy cavalry regiments at Waterloo, three (1st Dragoon Guards, 1st and 2nd Dragoons) wore dark blue facings and gold lace (yellow for the rank and file) while the 6th Dragoons wore yellow facings with silver lace (white for the rank and file). Some sources show the 1st Dragoon Guards wearing 'gauntlet'-type cuffs as worn by the Royal Horse Guards (Plate 2), but the officer illustrated here is copied from a contemporary portrait. The horse-furniture shown is typical of that used on campaign by the British cavalry in general, the more ornate full-dress housings being replaced by an assortment of equipment needed for active service, the individual regiments being distinguished by the lettering on the valise. The 1796 pattern heavy cavalry sabre was the regulation side-arm, but the officer in this plate is shown carrying a slightly unusual curved sabre. British officers were often a law unto themselves with regard to their uniform and equipment: in the period in question, for example, Captain Peters of the 9th Light Dragoons carried a sword of the 1803 infantry flank company pattern instead of the regulation issue.

The 1st (King's) Dragoon Guards, forming part of Lord Somerset's Brigade, was the strongest British cavalry regiment at Waterloo, with 530 men, of whom eleven officers and 264 other ranks became casualties. The 1st (Royal) Dragoons (not illustrated) and the 6th (Inniskilling) Dragoons formed, with the 2nd Dragoons, part of the famous 'Union' Brigade, so called from its composition of English, Scottish and Irish regiments. The 1st Dragoons sustained casualties of fourteen officers and 182 men out of 394, while the Inniskillings lost seven officers and 215 men out of 396. The 6th, according to Captain Mercer of the Royal Horse Artillery, 'presented a sad spectacle' after the battle: 'they had lost more than half their appointments. Some had helmets, some had none; many had the skull-cap, but with the crest cut or broken off; some were on their own large horses, others on little ones they had picked up; belts there were on some; many were without, not only belts, but also canteens and haversacks.' Upon the death of the Union Brigade's commander, Sir William Ponsonby, Lt.-Col. Muter of the 6th assumed command of the Brigade, though he himself 'had his helmet beaten in, and his arm, which had been badly wounded, was in a sling'. It is interesting to note that one of the 6th's officers was a Neapolitan, Lieutenant Paul Ruffo, Prince Castelcicala.

The 1st Dragoons captured one of the two French 'Eagles' taken by the Union Brigade, that of the 105th Regiment, taken by Captain Alexander Kennedy Clark and Corporal Francis Stiles. To commemorate the action, the Royal Dragoons wore a representation of the 'Eagle' as a badge until their amalgamation with the Royal Horse Guards in 1969.

4. Great Britain: Officer, 2nd (Royal North British) Dragoons. Sergeant, 2nd (Royal North British) Dragoons

The 2nd (Royal North British) Dragoons (Royal Scots Greys) wore the regulation Dragoon uniform, with the addition of their own unique head-dress, the bearskin cap. This was covered with an oilskin 'waterproof' on campaign; in full dress it was ornamented with a white plume and yellow cords. Some contemporary pictures show the plume worn on service, with its own small waterproof cover. At the rear was a red cloth patch, bearing the badge of the white horse of Hanover; officers' caps in addition had a small silver badge of the Star of the Order of the Thistle below the patch. The brass front-plate bore the Royal Arms. The jacket, styled like those of the other Dragoon regiments, had dark blue facings and gold lace (yellow for the rank and file). The regulation horse-furniture was carried, with the red cloak rolled across the front of the saddle, partly covered by a 'waterdeck'. The valise bore the 'R.N.B.D.' initials, signifying the regiment's title. The sergeant is shown wearing the haversack and canteen carried on campaign, in addition to the two shoulder-belts, one for the carbine and the other for the pouch.

The officer is shown in full dress, with white breeches and riding-boots. The girdle was common to all British cavalry regiments (the colours being varied), though a portrait of Captain Barnard of the 'Greys' in 1813 shows a plain crimson sash, probably worn as an alternative. According to some sources, the officers' turnbacks were fastened by a lace rosette with a button in the centre, a unique distinction. The sabre-tache was of plain black leather in all orders of dress, suspended from a white leather waist-belt, the plate of which bore an elaborate design of a Garter lettered 'Nemo Me Impune Lacessit', with a Crown overall and a Thistle in the centre, with 'G' and 'R' in the top two corners, and a wreath of roses and thistles underneath. It is probable that the rank and file of the 2nd Dragoons wore moustaches during the 1815 campaign.

The splendid uniform of the 'Greys', even before the battle, presented a sorry appearance, due to the inclement weather – Lieutenant Hamilton wrote that they were 'A miserable looking set of creatures – covered with mud from head to foot – our white belts dyed with the red from our jackets, as if we had already completed the sanguinary work, which we were soon about to begin.' Out of 396 men, the regiment suffered casualties of fourteen officers and 185 other ranks; their colonel, James Hamilton, was killed, and at the end of the action command had devolved upon a captain, Edward Cheney. That night, only sixteen of all ranks were mustered, the remainder having lost their horses or become scattered.

The actions of the Scots Greys have passed into legend; in particular, those of Sergeant Charles Ewart, who captured the 'Eagle' of the French 45th Regiment. Highest praise came from Napoleon himself: 'Qu'ils sont terribles, ces Chevaux Gris'.

5. Great Britain : Trooper, 7th (Queen's Own) Hussars. Officer, 10th (Prince of Wales's Own Royal) Hussars

The British Hussar regiments wore a uniform similar to that worn by Hussars throughout Europe, characterised by the braided, tailless jacket or 'dolman', and the fur-edged pelisse, worn either as a jacket, or hanging from the shoulder. The 7th Hussars trooper is shown wearing the Peninsular War uniform (1813–14); in 1815 they had blue facings, yellow lace and fur caps. The 10th Hussars wore scarlet shakos, those of the officers having silver lace, with gold rosettes and cords; the other ranks' shakos had white lace and caplines of mixed red and yellow. The dolman and pelisse were of the standard pattern, the officers' pelisse-fur being white or grey, and that of the men black. Dark blue facings replaced the red worn until 1814. The yellow braid (gold for officers) contained one regimental variation: a wide lace edging around the panels of braid, known in the regiment as 'the frame'. According to the paintings of Denis Dighton, the horse-furniture of the 10th consisted of sheepskins (black for officers and white for other ranks) borne over dark blue shabraques, the front corners of which were rounded, the rear pointed, with a plain yellow lace edge (gold for officers). The valise is shown in contemporary pictures as dark blue, with either a white edging and figure '10', or a yellow edging and a 'X' over 'RH'. The dark blue cloak was carried rolled across the front of the saddle.

Even before the commencement of the battle, the 7th, in common with many regiments, 'were so covered with mud that it was utterly impossible to distinguish a feature in their faces or the colour of the lace of their dress . . . in a deplorable condition, wet thro' and thro' and covered with mud' as Captain Verner wrote. Being engaged on the retreat from Quatre Bras as well as at Waterloo, the 7th suffered heavier casualties (ten officers and 192 other ranks out of 380) than the 10th, which lost eight officers and eighty-six men out of 390. According to Captain Verner, only one officer of the 7th came out of the battle on the same horse as he had entered it, Lieutenant O'Grady; all the remainder were either themselves wounded or had at least one horse killed under them. As part of Vivian's Brigade, the 10th only came into action on the evening of Waterloo, but performed with distinction in the final charge of the day.

6. Great Britain: Officer, 18th Hussars. Trooper, 15th (King's) Hussars

In Plate 6, the 15th Hussars trooper is shown in the shako without the waterproof cover. The red shako was adopted by the 15th in February and March 1813, though at the time of Waterloo it is possible that fur caps were worn. The regulation Hussar uniform was worn, with scarlet facings and white lace (silver for officers). The officers' shakos were gold-laced. Officers wore blue-grey overalls with two scarlet stripes down the outer seam. All the British Light Cavalry were armed with the 1796 pattern sabre, in addition to pistols and carbines. Officers, however, chose their own pattern of sword, which resulted in an assortment of regulation weapons, 'mameluke'-style sabres (as carried by the officer in this plate), and a selection of various non-regulation styles.

The 18th Hussar officer is taken from a contemporary picture, showing the closed collar and 'cossack'-style over-alls adopted after Waterloo; though the original picture post-dates Waterloo, it is of interest as showing the regimental distinctions worn in 1815 – white fac-ings and pelisse-fur, silver lace, and the unique blue busby-bag. Grey overalls were worn on campaign.

Neither regiment was as heavily en-gaged at Waterloo as were the regi-ments of heavy cavalry; the 15th suffered casualties of nine officers and seventy-four men out of 392, and the 18th two officers and 100 other ranks out of 396; in addition, the 18th lost two men on the retreat from Quatre Bras. At the close of the battle, however, the 15th were commanded by Captain Hancox, the officers senior to him all having fallen.

7. Great Britain: Officer, 11th Light Dragoons. Trooper, 12th (Prince of Wales's) Light Dragoons

The British Light Dragoon uniform, adopted in 1812, consisted of a bell-topped shako, a dark blue Polish-style jacket with 'plastron' lapels in the facing colour, and the universal 'over-alls' worn on campaign. However, numerous regimental variations existed.

It seems probable that on campaign, the lapels were buttoned over, and thus appeared dark blue, with a thin piping of the facing colour visible. A further concession to the rigours of campaign was the waterproof cover to the shako, covering all the ornaments; both the latter features can be seen on the figure of the 12th Light Dragoon trooper. The facing colours and lace of the regiments engaged at Waterloo were as follows: 11th, buff facings and silver lace (white for the rank and file); 12th, yellow with silver lace; 13th, buff with gold lace (yellow for the rank and file); 16th, scarlet with silver lace; 23rd, crimson with silver lace.

Both regiments illustrated had other regimental distinctions: the 11th wore a shako-badge of white metal numerals 'XI', and the 12th Light Dragoons had an unofficial dark blue pelisse. Though Dighton shows a trooper as illustrated, it is only certain that the officers wore this garment, with facings of yellow plush; according to Lieutenant Thomas Reed, these pelisses were worn at the battle.

The casualties of the 11th, 12th and 13th regiments were not excessive; the 11th lost six officers and sixty men out of 390, the 12th five officers and 106 other ranks out of 388, and the 13th ten officers and ninety-nine men out of 390. Included in the ranks of the 12th at Waterloo was Captain A. C. Crau-furd, a volunteer from the 2nd Ceylon Regiment! One of the most remarkable stories connected with the battle concerns

Lt.-Col. Frederick Ponsonby of the
12th. Wounded in both arms, Ponsonby
was knocked from his horse by a third
sabre-stroke, and speared by a French
lancer as he lay helpless. Ponsonby was
then roughly handled by a Tirailleur
who robbed him, and was in a pitiable
state when a French officer approached.
The Frenchman, showing great kind-
ness, made Ponsonby as comfortable as
possible, and gave him some brandy;
before leaving, the officer promised to
send help to the wounded Englishman.
Shortly after, a second Tirailleur came
up, and used poor Ponsonby as a shield
as he loaded and fired over him. Soon
after, two squadrons of Prussian cavalry
rode over him, and Ponsonby was again
maltreated and searched by a Prussian
scavenger. During the night, however,
a private of the 40th Foot – also looking
for plunder – came up and stood guard
over the colonel until help came next
morning. After a long convalescence,
Ponsonby recovered, and in 1827 met
the French officer who had saved his
life, the Baron de Laussat, who had been
a major in the Dragoons of the Imperial
Guard.

8/9. Great Britain:
Officer, Royal Horse
Artillery.
Gunner, Royal Horse
Artillery.
Gunner, Mounted Rocket
Corps.
Officer, Royal Foot
Artillery.

Private, Corps of Royal Artillery Drivers

This plate shows the uniforms of the
four branches of the Royal Artillery
present at Waterloo – the Royal Horse
Artillery, the Royal Foot Artillery, the
Mounted Rocket Corps, and the Corps
of the Royal Artillery Drivers.

The Royal Horse Artillery was uniformed in the pre-1812 Light Dragoon
style, with braided dolmans and the
'Tarleton' helmet. Although the officer
is depicted in this plate wearing
breeches and 'Hessian' boots, the more
usual style was the overalls, as worn by
the gunners. The pelisse was of Hussar
pattern, and was worn in service dress
as well as in full dress. There is some
doubt about the colour of the helmet-
turbans, as to whether they were dark
blue or black; though extant examples
of officers' helmets have black velvet
turbans. As usual among British officers,
some non-regulation styles were worn:
Captain Ramsay, for example, wore a
leather waist-belt instead of a sash.
Sabretaches were also carried in the
field. Captain Mercer described the
battle-stained appearance of his troop:
'My poor men . . . fairly worn out, their
clothes, faces, &c, blackened by the
smoke and spattered over with mud and
blood . . .'

The 2nd Troop of the Mounted
Rocket Corps was commanded by
Major E. C. Whinyates, and was
equipped with six-pounder cannon as
well as with the rockets, as Wellington
– with good reason – considered the

latter most unreliable. The uniform was similar to that of the Royal Horse Artillery, but with slightly different braiding on the dolman, plus a waist-belt. The shabraque bore the unusual cipher of 'G.P.R.', representing 'George, Prince Regent'. The rocket-poles had the distinctive pennon attached.

The Royal Foot Artillery was uni-formed in the infantry style, but in the artillery colours of blue with red facings. The head-dress was the 'Belgic' shako, shown here with its waterproof cover. Officers on occasion wore the lapels buttoned back to present a 'plastron'-style in the red-facing col-our. Lace of the rank and file was yellow, in 'bastion' shape.

The uniform of the Corps of Royal Artillery Drivers was a curious com-bination of Horse and Foot Artillery styles – 'Tarleton' helmets and overalls like the mounted branch, with Foot Artillery jackets.

The seven Foot Artillery batteries (only five were actually engaged) were armed with nine-pounder cannon; four of the R.H.A. troops were armed with nine-pounders also, while two (Gar-diner's and Webber Smith's) had six-pounders. Each of the troops also had one howitzer, and Bull's troop was equipped entirely with howitzers, which, instead of firing roundshot, fired spherical shell. In addition, Whinyates clung to his twelve-pound rockets, in spite of orders to relinquish them.

The Royal Artillery has never re-ceived full credit for its part in the battle; without doubt it contributed greatly to the Allied victory. Being the only part of the army engaged through-out, an immense number of rounds were fired: Sandham's Foot battery fired no fewer than 1,100, Mercer's 'G' Troop 700, and Webber Smith's 'F' Troop 670. Whinyates fired fifty-two rockets, with mixed success. One of the classic eye-witness accounts of the battle comes from Captain Mercer, who described with horror how wave after wave of French cuirassiers charged his six guns, squadron following squadron with incredible bravery until a ghastly rampart of bodies was built up at the very muzzles of Mercer's cannon. By pouring round after round of grape-shot and 'canister' (metal cans filled with musket-balls) into the French troops, many attacks were broken up before they came within musket range.

Losses were severe. Mercer, so proud of his troop, lost so many horses that he was unable to advance when the French began to retreat. Twenty-nine officers and 285 men were casualties. The Horse Artillery in particular suffered heavily: in 'I' Troop, Major Bull was wounded and his second-in-command killed, and he was forced to withdraw his guns be-fore the close of the battle due to heavy losses; Whinyates, his second captain, and two lieutenants were all wounded, and the command of the rocket detach-ment fell to an N.C.O., Sergeant Dunnet. In 'H' Troop, the famous Captain Norman Ramsey was killed, and only one officer left unwounded; Major Bean of 'D' Troop was killed. In the Foot Batteries, Captain Bolton was killed, and his second captain, Napier, received eight wounds when a shell exploded nearby; Major Lloyd died on 29 July, of a wound received at Waterloo.

10. Great Britain: Officer, 16th (Queen's) Light Dragoons. N.C.O., 23rd Light Dragoons

Plate 10 illustrates the pre-1812 light dragoon uniform. Regimental Inspection Returns state that both units wore regulation dress, i.e. as shown in Plate 7, though the tradition attached to an extant garment suggests that the old braided dolman was retained by at least one officer, perhaps with the old 'barrelled' sash. Apart from this (perhaps dubious) tradition and a written reference to another officer, there is no evidence that the old style was retained. The 23rd's old-style dress is shown by a contemporary painting and a print dated as late as 1818, but the more reliable Inspection Returns make no mention of any deviation from the regulation (i.e. 1812-style) dress. The sergeant shown in this plate wears the full dress white breeches and 'Hessian' boots.

Compared to other British cavalry regiments, neither suffered heavy casualties: the 16th lost six officers and twenty-six men out of 393 (of whom only ten were killed), and the 23rd seven officers and seventy-three men out of 387.

One of the saddest stories connected with the battle concerns Lieutenant-Colonel The Earl of Portarlington, commander of the 23rd Light Dragoons. On the evening before the action of 18 June, he unwisely went to Brussels, and returned too late to command his regiment. Instead, he attached himself to the 18th Hussars, and served with great bravery, having his horse shot from under him. However, the disgrace of not being present with his regiment caused him to resign from the 23rd, and, heartbroken, he took to dissipation, lost his fortune, and died prematurely in a London slum.

11. Great Britain: Officer, Battalion Company, 1st Foot Guards. Sergeant, Light Company, 2nd (Coldstream) Foot Guards

The Foot Guards were uniformed like the line infantry, but with regimental distinctions. They wore the 'Belgic' shako, usually covered in black oilskin, and the regulation scarlet jacket. Facings for all three regiments of guards were dark blue, with gold lace for the officers. Sergeants also wore gold lace, while that of the rank and file was white, in regimental patterns; the 1st Guards' lace was equally spaced, the

2nd's in pairs, and that of the 3rd in groups of three. The overalls *may* have been worn tucked into the gaiters, but the usual style is equally likely.

The officer of the Battalion Company of the 1st Guards illustrated wears the epaulettes which indicate his company; members of the Grenadier and Light companies wore 'wings'. The epaulette and turnback badges of the officers of the 1st Guards consisted of a Garter Star in embroidery and velvet. The broad gold-lace edging to the facings was a distinction reserved for Guards regiments.

The Sergeant of the Light Company of the 2nd Guards demonstrates the variations of uniform which indicated the company. The 'Belgic' shako (shown here without its usual cover) had the regimental-pattern plate, but with the addition of a bugle-horn badge, the symbol of Light Infantry; the green plume and 'wings' on the jacket also indicate the Light Infantry Company. Privates of this company wore green shako-cords (as different from the white worn by the remainder of the regiment); gold cords were reserved for sergeants. Officers wore the regulation gold and crimson cords, the Grenadier Company had white plumes, and the battalion companies white over red. The sergeants of the Foot Guards wore scarlet jackets, as distinct from the duller red of the rank and file. Sergeants' sashes usually carried a central stripe of the facing colour of the regiment, but those of the 2nd Guards were all crimson, like the officers'. The Guards wore the overalls tucked into their gaiters during the 1815 campaign. The equipment was regulation, with regimental distinction of the lettering 'Cm Gds' on the canteen, and the regimental device on the rear of the knapsack. Note the whistle carried by sergeants of the Light Company. Like the sergeants of the line infantry, those of the Foot Guards carried short sabres, though Light Company sergeants were armed with light muskets, the remainder carrying the 'spontoon' or half-pike.

The four Guards battalions (2nd and 3rd Battalions of the 1st Guards, and the 2nd Battalions of the 2nd and 3rd (Scots) Guards) played a decisive part in the battle. The successful defence of Hougoumont hinged upon the actions of Lt.-Col. Macdonell of Glengarry, Captain Wyndham, Ensigns Gooch and Hervey, and Sergeant Graham, of the 2nd Guards, who succeeded in closing the gate of the château when it had been forced by a party of French infantry. The 1st Guards were granted the title 'Grenadier' in memory of their defeat of the French Grenadiers of the Imperial Guard at a critical stage of the action; unfortunately for legend, the real credit for this victory should have gone to the 52nd Light Infantry, and the body of French troops involved were not the Guard Grenadiers in any case!

Casualties suffered by the four battalions on the three days of action were severe: the 1st Guards lost twenty-eight officers and 1,006 men out of 1,997; the 2nd eight officers and 300 men from 1,003; and the 3rd twelve officers and

234 men out of 1,061. The nine most senior officers of the 1st Guards were all casualties.

12. Great Britain: Sergeant, Light Company, 27th (Inniskilling) Regiment. Officer, Battalion Company 4th (King's Own) Regiment

British infantry battalions were composed of 'Battalion' or centre companies, plus two 'flank' companies, formed of Grenadiers and Light Infantry. The various companies were distinguished in the following way:

Battalion companies – white over red shako plumes; shoulder-straps with worsted tufts; officers wore epaulettes.

Grenadier companies – white plumes; red 'wings' with white fringes; officers wore laced or chain 'wings'.

Light companies – green plumes and shako-cords; 'wings' like the Grenadiers.

In addition, there were numerous variations on the above details. The basic infantry uniform adopted in 1812 consisted of the 'Belgic' shako, with or without the waterproof 'fall' at the back, a short-tailed jacket, and overall trousers. Officers' jackets were laced with either silver or gold; other ranks' lace was of white tape with a coloured design, in various patterns.

The officer of the 4th Regiment illustrated shows the shako without its normal waterproof covering; officers' cords were of mixed gold and crimson braid. Shako-plates frequently bore regimental devices (in this case a lion and the regimental number), though some regiments had the simple 'G.R.' cipher. Shoulder-belt plates likewise were of regimental pattern, varying from elaborate heraldic designs to simple regimental numbers. The type of metal varied according to the lace. Officers' lace of the 4th was gold; that of the other ranks was in 'bastion' shape, equally spaced, and bearing an interwoven blue stripe.

The Sergeant of the Light Company of the 27th (Inniskilling) Regiment is shown in a shako bearing the device of a bugle-horn over the regimental number, which was worn by the light companies of some regiments; unusually, the 27th's Light Company had white shako-cords. The lace worn by the 27th was set in square-ended loops, spaced equally, with the design of a red and blue stripe woven into the lace. The regimental facings were buff, borne on the collar, shoulder-straps, cuffs, and as a central stripe to the sergeants' sashes. The chevrons had a backing of the facing colour, and officers wore gold lace.

Out of a strength of 669, the 4th Foot suffered casualties of nine officers and 125 men; the Inniskillings were almost annihilated, losing sixteen officers and 483 men out of 698. Blown to pieces while standing in square, they were described after the action as 'lying dead in a square'; only three officers were standing at the end of the battle. Their act of being mown down without flinching is one of the most heroic incidents of the campaign.

13. Great Britain: Private, Battalion Company, 28th (North Gloucestershire) Regiment. Sergeant, Grenadier Company, 32nd (Cornwall) Regiment

The 28th (North Gloucestershire) Regiment was uniformed in the regulation style, with one exception: the 'Belgic' shako was not adopted in 1812, the regiment continuing to wear the old 'stovepipe' pattern. On this shako, the 28th wore their own badge, consisting of a crown surmounted by a lion, over the number '28', with a scroll bearing the honour 'Barrossa' above, and one bearing 'Peninsula' below. The rear of the head-dress was ornamented with a small diamond-shaped brass badge, commemorating the action at Alexandria when the rear rank of the 28th 'faced about' to repel an attack from the rear. This 'back badge' is still worn by the Gloucestershire Regiment. Another distinction was that the Grenadier Company, and perhaps others also, wore French hide knapsacks, which had been captured in Egypt. Their facings were 'bright yellow', and officers' lace silver; other ranks' lace was square-ended, in pairs, with a yellow stripe

between two black ones woven in. Out of a strength of 557 men, the 28th lost twenty officers and 232 men in the Waterloo campaign.

The 32nd (Cornwall) Regiment had white facings; officers' buttons were gilt, but they wore no lace. The lace of the other ranks was square-ended, and bore a black 'worm' and a black stripe. The sergeant is shown with his 'spontoon' or half-pike, carried by the Battalion and Grenadier Company sergeants. Out of 662 men, the 32nd suffered casualties of thirty-one officers and 339 other ranks, the majority of these being killed or wounded at Quatre Bras.

14. Great Britain: Private, Grenadier Company, 73rd (Highland) Regiment. Officer, Light Company, 33rd (1st Yorkshire West Riding) Regiment

The 33rd (1st Yorkshire West Riding) Regiment had red facings. The officer illustrated belongs to the Light Company, this being illustrated by his green shako-plume and the 'wings' on his jacket. In addition, the 33rd's Light Company bore the bugle-horn badge and regimental number on the front of the shako. The bugle-horn badge was repeated on the 'shell' of each wing. Further indications of the company were the sash of the corded Light Infantry pattern, and the 1803 pattern flank company sabre, carried in place of the straight-bladed sword of the Battalion companies. Other ranks' lace was 'bastion' shaped, in pairs, with a red stripe.

The 73rd (Highland) Regiment, in spite of its title, was uniformed as a line regiment. This figure shows the equipment carried by the British infantry: a black knapsack, often bearing the regimental badge or number; a black cartridge-box, a white haversack, and a light blue canteen. The greatcoat was rolled on top of the knapsack. All leather belts and straps were white (or whitened buff for those regiments with buff facings), except for the canteen-strap, which was dark brown. The regimental facings were dark green, and officers' lace was gold. The other ranks' lace was of 'bastion' shape, equally spaced, with a red stripe.

The 33rd, out of a total of 561, lost twenty-two officers and 269 men in three days of fighting; the 73rd, from 562 men, lost twenty-two officers and 214 men in the same time. At the end of the battle, only five officers of the 73rd were alive and unwounded, the senior being Lieutenant Leyne.

The basic uniform details of the British line regiments not illustrated are listed below:

1st (Royal Scots). Facings: blue. Officers' lace: gold. Other ranks' lace: bastion-shaped, equally spaced, with a blue stripe.

14th (Buckinghamshire) Regiment. Facings: buff. Officers' lace: none worn; buttons silver. Other ranks' lace: square-ended, in pairs, with one black and one red stripe.

23rd (Royal Welch Fuzileers). Facings: blue. Officers' lace: gold. Other ranks' lace: bastion-shaped, equally spaced, with red, blue and yellow stripes.

30th (Cambridgeshire) Regiment. Facings: pale yellow. Officers' lace: none worn; buttons silver. Other ranks' lace: bastion-shaped, equally spaced, with a pale blue stripe.

35th (Sussex) Regiment. Facings: orange. Officers' lace: silver. Other ranks' lace: square-ended, equally spaced, with red, yellow and blue stripes.

40th (2nd Somersetshire) Regiment. Facings: buff. Officers' lace: none worn; gilt buttons. Other ranks' lace: square-ended, in pairs, with black and red stripes.

44th (East Essex) Regiment. Facings: yellow. Officers' lace: none worn; buttons silver. Other ranks' lace: square-ended, equally spaced, with blue and black stripes.

54th (West Norfolk) Regiment. Facings: green. Officers' lace: silver. Other ranks' lace: pointed, in pairs, with a green stripe.

69th (South Lincolnshire) Regiment. Facings: green. Officers' lace: gold. Other ranks' lace: square-ended, in pairs, with one red and two green stripes.

91st (Argyllshire) Regiment. Facings: yellow. Officers' lace: silver. Other ranks' lace: square-ended, in pairs, with a black stripe and black 'darts'.

15. Great Britain: Officer, 51st (2nd Yorkshire West Riding) Light Infantry. Private, 52nd (Oxfordshire) Light Infantry

The Light Infantry were uniformed in a similar manner to the line, but retained the 'stovepipe' shako, which bore a bugle-horn badge and green plume. Officers were distinguished by 'wings', the curved flank company sabre, and the corded sash; other ranks wore 'wings' also. Instead of the standard 'Brown Bess' musket, the Light Infantry carried a slightly shorter, lighter version.

Three regiments of Light Infantry were engaged at Waterloo, of which two are illustrated here. The 51st (2nd Yorkshire West Riding) Regiment had grass green facings, officers' lace was gold, and that of the rank and file pointed, in pairs, with a green stripe. The 52nd (Oxfordshire) Regiment had buff facings, officers wore no lace but had silver buttons, and the other ranks' lace was square-ended, in pairs, with red, black and buff stripes.

The 51st, stationed on the extreme end of the Allied line, saw little action, and suffered only nine men killed, and two officers and twenty men wounded, out of 549. The 52nd, however, played a vital part in the closing stages of the battle. As Wellington ordered his Guards to 'stand up' in front of the advancing Imperial Guard, Lt.-Col. Sir John Colborne wheeled his 52nd Light Infantry to rake the flanks of the French formation with musketry; it was this, rather than the action of Maitland's Guards Brigade, which caused the French to break. The price of this decisive and brilliant action was severe – nine officers and 190 other ranks out of 1,038, of whom 140 fell while the wheeling movement was carried out. It says much of the bravery and discipline of this splendid battalion that so complicated a manoeuvre could be executed while being raked by artillery fire and musketry. The 52nd 'lost' (though not in the conventional sense) its King's Colour at Waterloo; Ensign William Nettles was killed while carrying the colour, and fell upon it; it was recovered from underneath his body on the following day.

16. Great Britain: Sergeant, 71st (Glasgow) Light Infantry. Field Officer, 42nd (Royal Highland) Regiment (Black Watch)

The third regiment of Light Infantry at Waterloo was the 71st (Glasgow Highland) Light Infantry. Their uniforms bore distinct traces of their Scottish origin – the dark blue shakos of the rank and file had a band of 'Highland dicing' around the base, although officers wore regulation black shakos. Officers and sergeants wore their sashes in the Highland style, over the shoulder rather than around the waist. Facings were buff, officers' lace silver, and the other ranks' lace square-ended, equally spaced, with a red stripe. The regiment also had bagpipers, a further indication of their 'Highland' descent. Sergeants carried short, light fusils instead of the standard Light Infantry musket. The last French cannon fired at Waterloo was one captured by a detachment of the 71st under Lieutenant William Torriano, who had the gun turned round and fired into the retreating French. The regiment lost fifteen officers and 184 men out of 810.

The 42nd (Royal Highland) Regiment (Black Watch) is without doubt one of the most famous regiments engaged in the 1815 campaign. The uniform was of the regulation 'Highland' style, but with regimental variations. The feather bonnet had a band of 'Highland dicing', and was worn with a detachable peak. The feather plumes were red for the Battalion companies, red over white for Grenadiers, red over green for the Light Company, and red over yellow for drummers. Under the plume was worn the cockade, black for Battalion companies, fastened by a button; green edged red and bearing a brass bugle-horn over a sphinx for the Light Company, red edged black with a sphinx over '42' for drummers, red with a grenade over a sphinx for the Grenadiers; officers of Battalion companies had black cockades fastened with a gilt sphinx, and Grenadier officers wore the grenade and sphinx alone, without a cockade. Jackets were of the regulation infantry pattern, with blue facings; officers' lace was gold, and that of the

rank and file bastion-shaped, equally spaced, with a red stripe. Sergeants had silver lace.

Kilts were worn by all ranks in campaign dress, except officers; sporrans were not worn on service. The tartan was of 'Government' pattern, now known as 'Black Watch'; the Grenadier Company had a similar sett, but with the addition of a red overstripe, while pipers wore kilts of Royal Stewart tartan. With the kilt were worn the hose, of a red and white checked pattern, the red bands having a black edging, over which were worn dark grey gaiters. Officers wore dark grey or blue overalls, with two red stripes down the outer seams.

Field officers carried infantry sabres, but Company officers, sergeants and pipers were armed with the broadsword, except sergeants of the Light Company, who carried regulation brass-hilted sabres instead.

At Waterloo, the 42nd were not heavily engaged, but had a most desperate battle at Quatre Bras, when they were partly overrun by French cavalry while in the act of forming square; total losses for the three days' action were twenty-four officers and 314 men out of 526. In the action at Quatre Bras, three successive commanding officers fell in a couple of minutes, including the Lt.-Col., Sir Robert Macara, who, being seriously wounded, was captured as he was being carried from the field, and then ruthlessly cut down. Of the fourteen most senior officers in the regiment, only one, Captain John Campbell, was unhurt. Major R. H.

Dick suffered sixteen wounds, and survived, while Captain Menzies of the Grenadier Company, who stood six feet six inches without his bonnet, took on a troop of lancers single-handed. He killed a large number with his broadsword, an ancient weapon made by Andrea Ferrara, before he fell with seventeen lance wounds. He lived to a great age, and enjoyed telling his dinner guests in Perthshire that of the seventeen wounds he received, fourteen were mortal!

17. Great Britain: Sergeant, Battalion Company, 79th (Cameron) Highlanders. Private, Grenadier Company, 92nd (Gordon) Highlanders

Both the 79th (Cameron) Highlanders and the 92nd (Gordon) Highlanders wore the standard 'Highland' dress, but with their own regimental distinctions. The 79th wore dark green facings, officers' lace was gold, and the other ranks' was square-ended, in pairs, with a yellow stripe between two red ones. Like the 42nd, the regiment's sergeants had silver lace. Bonnet-plumes were in the normal 'company' distinguishing colours, the cockades being fastened by a metal grenade and bugle-horn for the flank companies, Grenadiers and Light Infantry respectively. The tartan was 'Cameron of Erracht', basically the Macdonald sett, minus three red lines,

with the yellow Cameron overstripe. Officers wore grey overalls; some sources show these as having red stripes. The 92nd wore a similar costume, but with yellow facings, silver officers' lace with a black stripe, reputed to commemorate the death of Sir John Moore at Corunna in 1809; other ranks' lace was square-ended, in pairs, with a green stripe. Regimental Orders of the 92nd expressly forbade the addition of the detachable peaks to the bonnets, but it seems likely that some members of the regiment wore them. The Light Company wore red cockades; the black cockades of the Grenadier and Battalion companies were fastened with white metal sphinx badges. Warrant officers wore silver lace; the tartan was Gordon, which was the 'Government' sett with a yellow overstripe. Officers wore grey overalls; it seems likely that Field Officers wore grey breeches, 'Hessian' boots, and wore a plaid of regimental tartan over the shoulder.

Casualties suffered by these two regiments testified to their part in the campaign; both lost more at Quatre Bras than at Waterloo. In the three days, the 79th lost thirty officers and 448 men out of 703 and the 92nd twenty-six officers and 370 other ranks from a total of 558 men; at the close of the battle of Waterloo, the 79th were commanded by a junior Lieutenant, James Cameron. At Quatre Bras, the 92nd lost their Lieutenant-Colonel, the universally-popular John Cameron of Fassiefern, who was buried on 17 June in a shallow grave dug by his foster-brother, Ewen McMilland, who, in the old Highland tradition, had accompanied his master throughout his military career. Another notable character, who happily survived the battle, was Piper Kenneth MacKay of the Grenadier Company of the 79th, who, in the heat of the battle, marched round the *outside* of his regiment's square playing 'Cogadh No Sith'; he was presented with a set of silver pipes for his bravery.

One of the most famous incidents in the battle occurred when the Royal Scots Greys charged through the ranks of the 92nd, some of the Highlanders seizing the stirrup-leathers of the cavalry and being carried forward in the charge. The incident produced a number of stirring but quite unauthentic Victorian paintings.

18. Great Britain: Rifleman, 95th Rifles. Officer, 95th Rifles

Of all the regiments present at Waterloo, none was more famous at that time than the 95th Rifles. A highly-trained regiment of expert marksmen and skirmishers, they drew a grudging respect even from their enemies. The good-humour and impregnable morale which existed in this élite corps is transferred in the number of books written by members of the regiment, the most famous being the two by John Kincaid, the Adjutant of the 1st Battalion at Waterloo. Their effect on the Napoleonic Wars has never been truly judged – the presence of such a magnificently skilled corps in the Peninsular War was without doubt a considerable factor in the Allied victory.

The 95th wore the fabled 'rifle green' uniform, officers being dressed in the Hussar style, with dolman and pelisse braided in black; the pelisse had brown fur trim. Either Hussar-style 'barrel' sashes, or plain crimson sashes were worn by officers. Equipment was black leather, and the greatcoats were unusually white. (First Lieutenant George Simmons wore a white cloak at Waterloo – one he had stripped off a dead French cuirassier!). N.C.O.s' rank chevrons were in white lace. Apparently, several versions of the officers' shako existed, including one with a square-cut peak which could be folded back so that the shako, in silhouette, looked like a 'mirliton' cap.

The 95th were armed with the 'Baker' rifle and sword-bayonet; the standard of marksmanship was phenomenal. Officers were armed with a sword humorously described by Kincaid as 'our small regulation half-moon sabre . . . better calculated to shave a lady's-maid than a Frenchman's head'. In Kincaid's case at Waterloo, the effectiveness of his sword was of no consequence, as it had rusted solid in the scabbard due to heavy rain!

At Waterloo were the 1st and 2nd Battalions of the 95th, plus two companies from the 3rd Battalion. Total casualties were thirty-five officers and 482 men out of 1,322.

19. Great Britain: Officer, Royal Waggon Train. Officer, Royal Engineers

The Royal Waggon Train was responsible for the transport of supplies, some munitions, and for the rudimentary ambulance service. Though absolutely vital for the conduct of any campaign, their services have been largely and unjustly forgotten. Their uniform consisted of a Light Dragoon-style shako, and a braided dolman (worn by officers); other ranks wore an unbraided jacket. The rank and file wore Light Dragoon-style red girdles, with two blue stripes. The corps was armed and equipped as Light Dragoons.

The Royal Engineers, another important yet forgotten corps, played little part in the Waterloo campaign. However, Lt.-Col. J. C. Smyth, the senior officer at Waterloo, had surveyed the Mont-Sainte-Jean ridge in 1814, on Wellington's instructions, and it was largely due to his excellent plan that Wellington was able to deploy his forces so rapidly and advantageously. The Royal Engineers' uniform was like that of the infantry in cut, though the officers had long-tailed coats; the facings were of 'Garter blue', a shade lighter than the normal blue facing colour.

One notable feat of heroism concerned an unknown driver of the Royal Waggon Train, who calmly drove a cart full of ammunition through a storm of musketry and artillery fire to supply the 3rd Foot Guards defending Hougoumont. Without the ammunition he carried, it is unlikely that the château could have been held, yet his name is lost to posterity.

20. Great Britain: Officer, 2nd Light Dragoons, King's German Legion. Trooper, 1st Light Dragoons, King's German Legion

Raised in 1803, the King's German Legion was a basically Hanoverian corps in British service (King George III being Elector of Hanover); of the numerous 'foreign corps' in British pay, the Legion was without doubt the finest: few regiments have had so distinguished a record as that won by the K.G.L. in the Peninsular War. Composed of Infantry, Light Infantry, Light Dragoons, Hussars and Artillery, the following units were engaged at Waterloo: 1st and 2nd Light Dragoons; 1st, 2nd and 3rd Hussars; 1st and 2nd Light Battalions; 1st, 2nd, 3rd, 4th, 5th and 8th Line Battalions; Horse and Foot Artillery.

The Light Dragoons were uniformed in the style of their British counterparts, in blue uniforms with red facings; lace was yellow for the 1st Regiment and white for the 2nd, officers' lace being gold and silver respectively. An unusual distinguishing feature shown by some authorities was the drooping horsehair plume of the 2nd Regiment. The *History of the King's German Legion* by N. L. Beamish (1832) illustrates the curious shield-shaped sabretache with curved sides, while other contemporary sources show a more conventional shape. Full-dress sabretaches had a blue cloth face with silver-lace edging, bearing a Crown over the Royal Cipher, 'G.R.', over a scroll.

Brigaded with the 23rd Light Dragoons in Dörnberg's 3rd Cavalry Brigade, the casualties incurred at Quatre Bras and Waterloo were comparatively light, though the 1st Regiment lost over a quarter of its strength: fourteen officers and 127 men out of 462, while the 2nd Regiment lost eight officers and sixty-eight men out of 419 (including two officers and two troopers who became casualties on the retreat to Quatre Bras).

21. Great Britain: Trooper, 3rd Hussars, King's German Legion. Officer, 1st Hussars, King's German Legion

Numerous contemporary illustrations show conflicting details regarding the costume of the three King's German Legion Hussar regiments. The two uniforms illustrated are taken from Beamish (1st Hussars) and from C. Hamilton Smith's *Costume of the Army* (2nd Hussars). Basically, the uniform details were as follows:

1st Hussars: Busby with red bag; red facings with gold lace (yellow for rank and file).

2nd Hussars: Brown fur busby with black peak, red bag; white facings and gold lace (yellow for rank and file).

3rd Hussars: Light Dragoon shako, yellow facings with silver lace (white for rank and file).

The above, however, should only be used as a basic guide, as other reliable sources differ considerably; for example, the 3rd Hussars are shown wearing the busby, in some cases with a peak like that of the 2nd. In all probability the costume worn on 18 June 1815 was like that illustrated in Plate 21.

The 3rd Hussars suffered the heaviest casualties at Waterloo, though even these were light by comparison to others in the Anglo-Allied army, being twelve officers and 118 men out of 622, of whom only forty-four were killed; the 1st Hussars lost only one officer and nine men out of 493; only one of their casualties was killed, and the figure includes three men returned as 'missing' in the retreat from Quatre Bras.

The Artillery of the German Legion (not illustrated) was uniformed substantially like the various branches of the Royal Artillery, with only minor distinctions. Total casualties among the two Horse and one Foot Battery were seven officers and seventy men.

22. Great Britain: Officer, Battalion Company, 5th Line Battalion, King's German Legion.

Private, Grenadier Company, 8th Line Battalion, King's German Legion

The uniform and organisation of the line battalions of the K.G.L. conformed closely to that of the British infantry; facings were dark blue, the distinction of a 'Royal' regiment in the British Army. An unusual feature were the blue 'wings' worn by the flank companies, these being red in British regiments. Some contemporary sources show the knapsacks as being painted dark blue, sometimes with red lettering on the sides to identify the battalion, for example, '5 K.G.L.'. Lace was in pairs, the officers' being gold, and that of the other ranks square-ended, with (according to some sources) a blue stripe. Turnback badges, as in the British Army, varied considerably; an officer's jacket still in existence has a diamond-shaped blue patch, bearing a Crown over 'K.G.L.' over a laurel spray, all in gold embroidery. Shako-badges and shoulder-belt plates bore the regimental device of a Garter, with the battalion number usually within.

The six line battalions present at Waterloo had a total strength of 2,525 rank and file, from which they suffered casualties of thirty-six officers and 754 men. One of the most tragic incidents in the battle occurred when the Prince of Orange ordered Colonel von Ompteda, commander of the 2nd German Legion Brigade, to advance in support of the troops in La Haie Sainte. Ompteda

protested that they would be attacked by French cavalry, but Orange insisted that the 5th and 8th Line Battalions be deployed in line and advance. A strong force of French cavalry burst upon them, and overwhelmed the 8th Battalion, which almost ceased to exist as a fighting unit. Ompteda was killed, and the 5th Battalion only saved itself by forming square and retreating under cover of a charge by the remnants of the Household Brigade. A fine battalion had been thrown away for no reason.

23. Great Britain: Officer, 2nd Light Battalion, King's German Legion. Private, 1st Light Battalion, King's German Legion

The two Light Battalions of the German Legion were uniformed in a style approximating to that of the British rifle regiments, though with distinctive features. The 1st Light Battalion (illustrated) wore single-breasted jackets, with black worsted shoulder-rolls; the 2nd wore jackets with three rows of buttons on the breast, and black shoulder-straps with black worsted tufts, in shape like those of the British battalion companies. Both wore the 'stovepipe' shako, the 1st with a black plume, and the 2nd with a black ball-pompom. Facings were black in both cases. Officers of the 1st Battalion wore unbraided jackets, but those of the 2nd had braided dolmans. The officer illustrated is a 'reconstruction' from a uniform still in existence; the shako had a folding peak, resembling a 'mirliton' cap in shape. The gilt badge consisted of a Garter inscribed 'King's Germans', with a bugle-horn and the figure '2' inside. The yellow cockade was another unusual feature, as was the light green lacing on the overalls. Belts and equipment were of black leather for both battalions; one source shows a small badge painted on the side of the knapsack, consisting of a bugle-horn over the battalion number, all in green. Both battalions were armed with the 'Baker' rifle. Field Officers probably wore low black bicorn hats, with green plumes.

Both Light Battalions were engaged at Waterloo; they gained eternal fame for the defence of La Haie Sainte by the 2nd Light Battalion under Major Baring, supported by the 1st Light Battalion and the Light Company of the 5th Line Battalion. The defenders held the French off the walls of the farm until their ammunition was expended, then fought on with bayonet and rifle-butt until they were almost wiped out: only Major Baring and forty-two men were able to escape. Total casualties for the Light Battalions were twenty-six officers and 321 other ranks out of 860.

24/25: Hanover: Officer, Feld-Battalion Bremen. Officer, Luneburg Light Battalion. Sergeant, Grubenhagen Light Battalion

Private, Feld-Battalion Verden. Field Officer, Grubenhagen Light Battalion.

King George III being Elector of Hanover, the German state consequently provided a detachment for Wellington's force. The infantry battalions of Bremen, Verden, York, Lüneburg, Grubenhagen, Lauenburg, Calenburg and Hoya were present at the battle of Waterloo.

Uniform and equipment was in most respects like those of the British infantry, there being only minor differences; some sources show the plume worn at the front of the 'Belgic' shako by some of the battalions, and in addition most of the officers' sashes were yellow, though there is evidence that some British-style crimson ones were also worn. Some of the battalions were not equipped as fully as their British counterparts, a folded blanket having to suffice in place of the knapsack in some cases.

Two of the battalions illustrated in Plate 24/25 were light infantry, those of Lüneburg and Grubenhagen. Prior to 1814 the 'Belgic' shako was worn by the Lüneburg Light Battalion, but was replaced in that year by a 'stovepipe' version. The cornflower-blue overalls were worn only by officers; the other ranks wore either white or grey trousers, with black gaiters. The conical, peakless shako worn by the Grubenhagen Light Battalion was most unusual; the black bicorn was worn as an alternative by officers.

The Lauenburg and Calenburg Battalions were not engaged, but the other five battalions, from a total strength of 2,868, suffered casualties of thirty-eight officers and 852 men.

26. Hanover: Officer, Bremen and Verden Hussars. Trooper, Duke of Cumberland's Hussars

Three regiments of Hanoverian Hussars were present in the Waterloo campaign, the Duke of Cumberland's, the Prince Regent's and the Bremen and Verden Regiments. Their uniforms incorporated all the traditional features of Hussar costume; the Prince Regent's Regiment (not illustrated) wore brown fur busbies with blue bags and white plumes, blue dolmans faced scarlet, with silver lace, and scarlet pellisses edged with grey fur.

The Duke of Cumberland's Regiment brought disgrace upon all the Hanoverians present at Waterloo; at a critical time in the action, the whole regiment turned tail, abandoned the field entirely, and rode off to Brussels with the news that Wellington was defeated. The remainder of the Hanoverians behaved with great credit, but this corps, composed entirely of wealthy volunteers who furnished their own horses, disgraced both themselves and their countrymen. As a punishment, the regiment was broken up and distributed among various Allied corps to be employed as forage escorts and in other routine tasks. A corporal and four troopers were posted to Captain Mercer's Troop of the Royal Horse Artillery; he found them 'amazingly sulky and snappish with everyone . . .'

27. Hanover: Officer, Landwehr. Private, Landwehr

The Hanoverian Landwehr, a militia force raised on a local basis, was formed in 1814. Their uniform and equipment were hastily made, and consequently the Landwehr in many cases was severely short of accoutrements; hardly any, for example, were issued with bayonets. The uniform was based upon the British infantry pattern, though with the Hanoverian distinctions of yellow sashes for officers, and officially white over yellow plumes. The rank and file wore outdated 'stovepipe' shako with British-style plumes, though the officers wore the 'Belgic' cap.

The following Landwehr battalions were present with the Anglo-Allied army:

3rd Hanoverian Brigade: Battalions Bremervörde, Osnabrück, Quackenbrück, Salzgitter.

6th Hanoverian Brigade: Battalions Nienburg, Hoya, Bentheim.

5th Hanoverian Brigade: Battalions Hameln, Gifhorn, Hildesheim, Peine.

4th Hanoverian Brigade: Battalions Verden, Lüneburg, Osterode, Münden.

Hanoverian Reserve Corps: Battalions

Mölln, Bremerlehe, Nordheim, Ahlefeldt, Springe, Otterndorf, Zelle, Ratzeburg, Hanover, Uelzen, Neustadt, Diepholz.

Heaviest casualties were suffered by the Verden Battalion, which was overrun by French cavalry at Quatre Bras in the act of forming square, and was almost cut to pieces, losing six officers and 153 men.

28. Hanover: Officer, Foot Artillery. Private, Foot Artillery

The Hanoverian artillery wore British-style uniforms, with very few distinctions. The officer illustrated in Plate 28 shows how the lapels of the jacket could be buttoned back to present a scarlet 'plastron' effect; officers of the British Foot Artillery wore their jackets in this style on occasion also. On the private's cross-belt can be seen a brass match-case, and on the same belt a scarlet flask-cord.

Two batteries of Foot Artillery were present with Wellington's army; casualties suffered totalled two non-commissioned officers and thirty-three gunners.

29. Brunswick: Officer, Lancer Squadron. Trooper, Hussar Squadron

In 1814 Duke Friedrich Wilhelm of Brunswick disbanded his famous 'Black Legion' that had enlisted in British service in 1809 and fought throughout the Peninsular War. In its place, he raised a new national army, based on a nucleus of Peninsular veterans. Upon Napoleon's return from Elba the Duke offered his services immediately and joined Wellington's army with his 'Brunswick Corps'.

The cavalry of the Brunswick Corps consisted of a regiment of Hussars (690 men) and a squadron of Uhlans (232). The uniform for both was black, with sky-blue facings. The death's head badge prominently displayed on the head-dress and accoutrements of the Brunswick Corps enhanced their sombre appearance, which prompted Lady de Lancey to compare the Corps to 'an immense moving hearse'. The czapka worn by the officer of the Uhlan squadron illustrated was the old yellow cloth pattern worn prior to 1814, but which was also worn in the 'Hundred Days' campaign; the Uhlan troopers wore czapkas with light blue cloth tops. Their uniform contained all the traditional features of the arm of service, including the 'plastron' lapels. In place of the sash, Uhlan troopers wore light blue girdles with a central black stripe. The Hussar officers' sabretaches bore large white metal skull and crossed bones badges; lance-pennons of the Uhlan squadron were light blue over yellow.

Shabraques for the Uhlans were black, with rounded front and pointed rear corners; the troopers' shabraques were edged with a single band of light blue, those of the officers having a double band. Hussar officers used the same pattern of shabraque as the Uhlans, but the Hussar troopers had black sheepskins edged with light blue cloth in a 'wolf's tooth' pattern. All the cavalry had black valises, edged with light blue.

Both units of cavalry were engaged at Quatre Bras, the casualties of the Hussars being four officers and forty-two men, and the Uhlans fourteen other ranks.

30. Brunswick: Private, Leib-Battalion. Private, Avant-Garde Battalion

The Avant-Garde Battalion was a corps of sharpshooters, composed of four companies, two of 'Gelernte Jäger' and two of light infantry; the illustration shows a member of the 'Gelernte Jäger'. The hat apparently existed in two versions; a number of sources show the right-hand side of the brim turned up, but an actual head-dress still in existence has the left-hand side turned up. Points of note in this uniform are the rifle and 'hirschfanger' or sword-bayonet. N.C.O.s had silver rank chevrons copied from the British pattern, and officers had silver lace on the hat, jacket and overalls; they were further distinguished by yellow and silver sashes, Hussar-style sabres, and (if of Field rank, i.e. Major and upwards) a Hussar-style pouchbelt. Their hat-plume was of green feathers. The light

infantry companies of the Avant-Garde wore the same type of hat, but with a white metal hunting-horn badge in place of the running horse; they wore black dolmans with dark green collar, cuffs and shoulder-straps, with the breast of the dolman braided in black. Trousers and gaiters were also black, the former having a dark green stripe down the seam.

The Leib-Battalion was uniformed in the standard Brunswick infantry fashion, being distinguished by sky-blue facings, and the drooping black horsehair plume; the skull and crossed bones device was repeated on the shako.

Both units were engaged at Quatre Bras; the Avant-Garde lost four officers and fifty-two men out of 672, and the Leib-Battalion five officers and 121 men, also from 672. The Leib-Battalion, being a newly-raised corps with a few Peninsular veterans in their ranks, unfortunately gave way at Quatre Bras in the face of heavy artillery fire; it was while he was trying to rally them that the Duke of Brunswick received his mortal wound.

31. Brunswick: Officer, 1st Line Battalion. Sergeant, 3rd Light Battalion

There were six regiments of infantry in the Brunswick Corps, three of line infantry and three of light. The uniforms were basically alike, though there were a number of distinguishing features. The shako of the line battalions had a plume of light blue over yellow, with a crescent-shaped plate bearing the running horse, the regimental number, and the motto 'Numquam Retrorsum'; the light infantry had plumes of yellow over light blue, and bugle-horn badges. There is evidence that some of the shakos were of the Russian-style scuttle-shaped 'kiwer' pattern, but in all probability the bell-topped version shown in this plate was the more common. The regiments were distinguished by the facing colours (worn on the collar, shoulder-straps and trouser-stripes) as follows:

1st Line Battalion: red
2nd Line Battalion: green
3rd Line Battalion: white
1st Light Battalion: pink
2nd Light Battalion: yellow
3rd Light Battalion: orange

Officers wore the standard yellow and silver sashes, and carried swords. Buglers were distinguished by 'swallow's nest'-type wings of the Prussian style, laced white.

Each battalion had a strength of 672; according to the official casualty returns, the infantry suffered the following casualties: 1st Line Battalion, 177; 2nd, 220; 3rd, 113; 1st Light Battalion, 71; 2nd, 203; 3rd, 270. The Brunswickers behaved reasonably well, but being almost all new recruits were generally somewhat unsteady. Kincaid remarks that they had a disconcerting habit of firing at anyone not wearing a Brunswick uniform, repeatedly blazing away at Allied skirmishers! Though, to their credit, Mercer praises their courage in standing firm when subjected to a very heavy fire, though the officers and N.C.O.s had to push and thump the privates in order to fill the gaps which appeared in the ranks; their steadiness was surprising, for Mercer noted that three days before, the same troops had flung away their arms and fled 'at the very sound of our horses' feet'!

32. Brunswick: Duke of Brunswick. Officer, Foot Artillery

Plate 32 shows the costume worn by the Duke of Brunswick at Quatre Bras; it basically consisted of a 'Polrock' worn over a braided coatee, with leather-strapped overalls, and an undress Hussar cap. The Duke behaved with conspicuous gallantry at Quatre Bras, repeatedly exposing himself to the enemy fire in an effort to raise the morale of his unsteady corps. At 6 p.m. the Leib-Battalion broke and fled, and, as he was trying to rally them, the 'Black Duke' was shot through the body and died within minutes. With the death of their leader, the morale of the Brunswick Corps sank to a lower ebb, and their performance at Waterloo was perhaps less than satisfactory. After Quatre Bras, command devolved upon Oberst Wachholtz.

The Brunswick Artillery was uniformed in the customary style, with black facings and yellow trimming.

Gunners of the Foot Artillery wore yellow tufts on the front of their shakos. Horse Artillery wore basically the Hussar uniform, with a white metal badge of the skull and crossed bones on the shako. Drivers of the Train of the Horse Artillery wore the same uniform, but drivers of the Train of the Foot Artillery had brownish-grey uniforms, faced black and trimmed with yellow. Cavalry sabres were carried by the Horse Artillery.

Total casualties in the campaign of the two batteries and their Train companies amounted to only twenty, of whom only two were killed.

33. Netherlands: Staff Officer. The Prince of Orange

The Prince of Orange, a Major-General in the British Army, and heir to the throne of the Netherlands, commanded the entire Anglo-Allied army until the Duke of Wellington's arrival, and was thereafter second-in-command. This was a 'diplomatic' appointment rather than one on merit, as the twenty-three-year-old prince was in no manner the ideal deputy to Wellington; indeed, it has been said that he was incapable of managing a single battalion, a judgement which is perhaps a little harsh. It is true, however, that some of Wellington's experienced Peninsular staff would have been far better suited for this important appointment. The Prince's command came to an abrupt end when he was wounded on 18 June.

Plate 33 shows the uniform worn by the Prince of Orange at Waterloo, taken from a portrait and from the actual garments. An unusual feature is the scabbard of his mameluke-hilted sabre, which was covered in red velvet, the hilt and scabbard-fittings being gilt. The simple horse-furniture, without shabraque, is that shown in the contemporary portrait.

The staff officer is shown wearing the regulation uniform, modified for wear on campaign; in full dress, white breeches replaced the overalls, and the hat had an edging of white feathers, and a white plume. A painting of the Prince and staff at Quatre Bras shows an aide-de-camp wearing a bell-topped shako with black plume, a grey, knee-length, double-breasted frock-coat with red collar, grey overalls, and the customary orange sash.

34. Netherlands: Trumpeter, 2nd (Belgian) Carabiniers. Trooper, 1st (Dutch) Carabiniers

Plate 34 shows the uniforms most likely to have been worn at Waterloo by the three regiments of Netherlands Carabiniers; it is possible that the old double-breasted coatee and white-plumed bicorn were retained by some, though these had been replaced by the 1815 Regulations.

The 1st (Dutch) Carabiniers wore single-breasted dark blue jackets, with pink facings; the 1815 Regulations had prescribed red, but the 1st Regiment retained their old facing colour; the yellow grenade badges of the turnbacks were also a non-regulation feature. The 2nd (Belgian) Regiment wore double-breasted blue jackets, with red lapels, which were folded back in service dress to show a red piping only. The 3rd (Dutch) Carabiniers wore a uniform like that of the 1st, but with yellow facings. Officers were distinguished by silver epaulettes, an orange waist-sash, and by more ornate decorations on the helmet; helmet-plumes were sometimes removed on active service. White breeches were worn in full dress, the grey ones being reserved for campaign; occasionally, grey overalls replaced the breeches. Officers were supposed to have black leather equipment, but most contemporary illustrations show white.

The Trumpeter illustrated in Plate 34 is typical of a style prevalent throughout Europe, the wearing of 'reversed colours' (i.e. the body of the coat in the regimental facing colour) or other distinctive patterns by musicians and trumpeters. In this case, the Trumpeter's coat was of the regimental facing, red, with the remainder in blue. An additional distinction, also common in many European armies, was the white woollen crest and distinctive red plume on the helmet.

Shabraques were similar for all Carabinier regiments, though those of the 2nd bore lace grenade badges in the rear corners and on the ends of the valise.

Casualties sustained in the campaign were not excessive; the 1st Regiment lost eleven officers and ninety-one other ranks from a total of 446, the 2nd five officers and 151 men out of 399, and the 3rd two officers and sixty-one men from 392.

35. Netherlands: Gunner, Foot Artillery. Officer, Horse Artillery

Four foot batteries and three horse batteries were present in the Waterloo campaign. The gunner of Foot Artillery shown in Plate 35 has the earlier pattern of shako, which was worn (in all probability) at Waterloo. Later in the year the shako authorised by the 1815 regulations was adopted, this having a larger plate embossed with a flaming grenade, and with the red-tipped black plume also worn on the previous pattern.

In full dress, the Horse Artillery wore grey breeches with a red stripe down the seam, and black 'Hessian' boots with black lace and tassels; on campaign these were replaced by grey overalls, those of the rank and file having black leather strapping and red stripes. Gunners wore a uniform basically similar to those of the officers, but with red shoulder-rolls with yellow piping, white belts with brass fittings, and red shako-cords. Trumpeters wore a most striking uniform, consisting of red jacket with black facings, and black epaulettes with yellow lace and fringe; one source shows this uniform worn with a black fur busby.

The Artillery Train wore shakos of a

similar pattern to those of the Foot Artillery, but with white metal plates consisting of a crown over crossed cannons, and a black plume; their jackets were grey with black collar, cuffs, and cuff-flaps, and grey shoulder straps, all piped red, with red turnbacks and white metal buttons. Overalls were worn like those of the Horse Artillery. Drivers of the Artillery Train were armed with sabres like the Horse Artillery, suspended from black leather waist-belts.

Total losses for the various artillery corps in the three days' action were seven officers and 195 men, of whom all the officer casualties and 111 of the other ranks were sustained by the Artillery Train of the 2nd (Netherlands) Division; this company also lost 114 horses.

36. Netherlands: Flanquer, Dutch Infantry. Officer, Dutch Infantry

The infantry of the Netherlands Army consisted of Dutch, Belgian, Nassau and Swiss mercenary troops. Plate 36 illustrates the uniform of the Dutch regiments. An infantry battalion consisted of six Fusilier companies (eight in the Swiss regiments) and two companies of 'Flanquers' (one equivalent to Grenadiers, the other to Light Infantry).

The shako worn by the Dutch battalions was the bell-topped pattern; the plume was white for Fusilier companies, and white with a coloured tip for the 'Flanquers': red for the heavy (Grenadier) companies, and green for the light companies. Fusilier companies were further distinguished by dark blue shoulder-straps piped white, while the 'Flanquers' wore shoulder-rolls of the same colours. Officers' coats were long-tailed. Facings were white for all regiments.

Overalls were officially white for summer, though it seems possible that the grey winter issue were also in use during the Waterloo campaign; these could be worn tucked into the gaiters, or worn outside. The grey overcoat worn rolled over the shoulder of the officer in Plate 36 was a style common to many armies; the thick roll provided a protection against sword-cuts, besides being the easiest way to carry the bulky greatcoat. The other ranks carried hide knapsacks, similar to the French pattern; canteens were light blue, British style.

The Dutch regiments present in the Waterloo campaign were those numbered 3rd, 6th, 12th and 13th; the three regiments actually engaged, the 3rd, 12th and 13th, sustained a total of one officer and 163 other ranks casualties, of whom only nine were killed and fifty-six wounded, the remainder being reported 'missing', a convenient way of describing desertion.

37. Netherlands: Grenadier Corporal, Belgian Infantry. Officer, Belgian Infantry

The Belgian infantry wore a uniform similar to that of the Dutch, but with the distinctive 'Belgic' shako in the British style. This had plume and cords in the 'company' colours – white for Fusiliers, red for the heavy (Grenadier) company of Flanquers, and green for the light Flanquer company. Officers wore the universal orange sash, and gold shako-cords. The shoulder-rolls worn by the Flanquers were similar to those of the Dutch infantry, but musicians and drummers of the Belgians wore wings of the the 'swallow's nest' style, of the facing colour with yellow lace. One source shows a drum-major in a brown fur busby with red bag and ball-pompom; the drum-major's baldric was white with a gold lace edging, and the rank was further distinguished by gold lace on the collar. Rank distinctions for the Netherlands Army were as follows:

Colonel: two epaulettes of the button colour (i.e. either gold or silver).

Lieutenant-Colonel: two epaulettes, with a stripe of the opposing metal down the strap (i.e. silver on gold).

Major: as Lieutenant-Colonel, but with two stripes down each strap.

Captain: one epaulette on the right shoulder, with heavy bullion fringe.

Lieutenant: as the Captain, but with light fringe.

Adjutant: as the Lieutenant, but epaulette on the left shoulder.

Sergeant-Major: double chevron of gold or silver lace above the cuff.

Sergeant: single chevron as above.

Corporal: double chevron of yellow or white lace.

Private 1st class: single chevron of the facing colour.

Officers' sword-knots were silver or gold, sergeants' silver with an orange knot, and corporals' white with orange knot. Short sabres were usually carried by N.C.O.s though the corporal illustrated is not carrying one.

The 1st, 2nd, 4th and 7th (Belgian) Regiments were present in the Waterloo campaign, of which only the 2nd and 7th were engaged, losing four officers and eighty-seven other ranks, and seven officers and 234 other ranks respectively out of respective totals of 471 and 701.

38. Netherlands: Officer, 16th Jägers, Centre Company. Hornist, 36th Jägers, Flanquer Company

There were six regiments of Jägers in the Netherlands Army; they wore uniforms of a similar cut to those of the infantry, but in the distinguishing colours of green with yellow facings as befitted a light infantry corps. The Dutch regiments wore the bell-topped shako, and the Belgian units the 'Belgic' pattern. The plumes of the Dutch regiments were in the company distinguishing colours of green for 'centre' companies, green tipped red for the heavy 'Flanquer' companies, and green tipped yellow for the light company. The shakos of Belgian regiments had plumes of distinguishing colours like those of the infantry. 'Flanquer' companies wore shoulder-rolls of green piped with the facing colour; musicians wore 'swallow's nest' wings of yellow with yellow lace. The hornist illustrated, being a member of the heavy 'Flanquer' company of the 36th Jägers, is shown wearing both wings and shoulder-rolls. Officers wore long-tailed coats, as in the infantry, with similar rank distinctions. Equipment was of the standard pattern, but with belts of black leather.

The 16th, 18th and 27th Dutch Jägers, and the 35th and 36th Belgian Jägers, served in the Waterloo campaign. The 27th, 35th and 36th were actively engaged in the three days' battle, sustaining total casualties of twelve officers and 464 men, of which the 27th lost no less than nine officers and 342 other ranks out of 809; being part of Bylandt's brigade in such an exposed position at Waterloo, it is easy to understand why their losses were so heavy, though it is surprising that only fifteen of all ranks were killed.

39. Netherlands: Officer, 5th National Militia. Private 1st Class, 19th National Militia

There were forty-five battalions of National Militia, which wore a variety of uniforms, based upon the regulation infantry style. Generally, the dark blue uniforms had orange facings; officers wore the bell-topped Dutch-style shako, while the other ranks had conical British-style head-dress, with an assortment of plates, these being in the shape of a 'sunburst' design, with either the Royal Cipher 'W', the battalion number, or a motto 'Voor Koning en Vaderland'. Other distinctions were like those of the regular infantry, though several sources show unique variations.

The 5th National Militia (illustrated) wore dark blue cuffs with orange piping, and the shako-plates bore the battalion number; the orange stripe on the epaulettes of the officer is another unusual feature. One source shows a light 'Flanquer' with green epaulettes which have red crescents, instead of the regulation shoulder-rolls, and a green over red plume; a heavy 'Flanquer' is shown with a white over red plume. Though cuffs were officially without flaps, some contemporary pictures show infantry-style cuffs in use. Being short of equipment in some cases, some units apparently wore Prussian-style peaked cloth caps, of dark blue with an orange band and piping around the top. Equipment, though supposedly of the regulation infantry style, did vary on occasion. Canteens bore the battalion identification in white letters, for example 'N.M. BN 19'.

The 1st, 2nd, 3rd, 4th, 5th, 6th, 7th, 8th, 9th, 10th, 14th, 15th, 17th, 18th and 19th battalions served in the Waterloo campaign, of which the 3rd, 4th, 5th, 6th, 7th, 8th, 10th, 17th and 19th were actively engaged, losing a combined total of thirty-six officers and 1,071 other ranks, though a large proportion of these were returned as 'missing'. The 5th Battalion, part of Bylandt's unfortunate brigade, suffered the most fatalities of any Netherlands unit, three officers and seventy other ranks.

40/41. Netherlands: Trooper, 4th (Dutch) Light Dragoons.
Officer, 5th (Belgian) Light Dragoons.
Trooper, 6th (Dutch) Hussars.
Officer, 8th (Belgian) Hussars.
N.C.O., Guides te Paard

The four light cavalry regiments present in the Waterloo campaign were the 4th (Dutch) Light Dragoons, 5th (Belgian) Light Dragoons, 6th (Dutch) Hussars and 8th (Belgian) Hussars. Although their uniforms incorporated many of the traditional light cavalry styles, all had unique distinguishing features.

The 4th (Dutch) Light Dragoons wore a jacket called a 'Karoko', of dark blue with red facings and white lace, and three rows of buttons on the breast. Officers wore similar jackets, but with silver lace, and some sources show their overalls as dark blue with a red stripe down the seam. Officers of the 4th were further distinguished by silver epaulettes, silver-laced belts, and the regulation orange-sash. Their shako-ornaments were silver, and some sources show the shield-shaped plate worn by

other ranks as replaced by a silver badge of the crowned 'W' cipher. Officers' shako-plumes were black with a white tip. Trumpeters of the 4th wore red Karokos, faced blue, with white braid, and either red shoulder-straps edged blue, or blue epaulettes edged with silver lace, with a mixed silver and white fringe.

The 5th (Belgian) Light Dragoons were raised in 1814 as the Chevau-légers of the Belgian Legion. Officers wore the French-style 'stovepipe' shako, and double-breasted green jackets with yellow facings, the cuffs being pointed. Other ranks wore 'bell-topped' shakos of green cloth, with white lace around the top, white cords, and a white metal crowned 'W' cipher on the front. Plumes were black with a yellow tip. Their jackets were similar to those of the officers, but with green shoulder-straps, piped yellow. Overalls were light grey, with green stripes down the outer seams. Equipment was of white leather. Shabraques were of the same pattern as those of the 4th Light Dragoons, but of dark green, edged yellow; sheepskins were white with a yellow 'wolf's tooth' edge. Officers' shabraques were the same, but with a silver lace edge, being used either without a sheepskin or with a black one. Trumpeters of the 5th wore single-breasted yellow jackets, with green facings, and yellow shoulder-straps piped green.

The 6th (Dutch) Hussars trooper (illustrated) shows the field dress worn by all the light cavalry regiments, characterised by the waterproof shako-cover and rolled greatcoat. The shako in full dress had a brass crowned 'W' plate, yellow lace band around the top, cords of mixed black and yellow, and a black plume. The dolman was light blue throughout, and in full dress a dark blue pelisse with black fur edging and the mixed yellow and black braid was worn. The full dress light blue breeches with 'Hessian' boots with black trim and tassels were replaced on campaign by the overalls illustrated. Trumpeters wore red dolmans with light blue facings.

The 8th (Belgian) Hussars were raised in 1814 as the 'Hussards de Croy'. The cylindrical shako was worn only by officers, the other ranks wearing a 'bell-topped' version like that of the 6th. The pelisse may have been worn by officers on campaign, though those of the rank and file were reserved for full dress. On campaign, light grey overalls with black leather strapping and two red stripes down each leg replaced the breeches. The regiment wore black leather belts. Shabraques were of a similar style to those of the 6th Hussars, but of light blue with a wide white lace border, piped around the outside in red. Sheepskins were white with a red 'wolf's tooth' edge. Officers' shabraques were light blue, edged silver, with the crowned 'W' cipher in silver in the rear corners, and without sheepskins. Trumpeters of the 8th wore red dolmans with light blue facings, red cloth shakos with white plumes, and red pelisses with brown fur. Trumpeters' braid was white, like that of the rank and file.

A further unit of cavalry was the 'Guides te Paard', formed to act as a bodyguard to the Commander-in-Chief in February 1815. On campaign, the breeches were replaced by grey over-alls with black leather strapping and a red stripe down each outer seam. Their shabraques were dark blue, with white lace edging, and no sheepskins; valises were also dark blue, laced white. The chevrons of N.C.O. rank (in this case sergeant) can be seen above the gauntlet-cuff.

The Netherlands Light Cavalry sustained heavy casualties, the 4th losing thirteen officers and 236 men out of 647, the 5th two officers and 155 other ranks from 441, the 6th nine officers and 205 from 641, and the 8th seven officers and 227 from 439; of these, eighty-seven of all ranks were killed.

42. Netherlands: Private, Netherlands Indian Brigade. Sergeant, 2nd Nassau Regiment

The Netherlands Indian Brigade of Lt.-Gen. Anthing comprised the 5th (East Indies) Infantry Regiment, a composite battalion of 'Flanquers' drawn from other infantry corps, and the 10th and 11th Indies Light Infantry. It would appear that the uniform worn by the Indies infantry was as shown in Plate 42, with the distinctive light blue facings and yellow lace loops.

King William I of the Netherlands was also Grand Duke of Nassau, and in consequence the 1st and 2nd Nassau Regiments and the Regiment of Orange Nassau joined the Netherlands Army and fought in the Waterloo campaign. Each Nassau regiment consisted of three battalions, each battalion comprising four Fusilier companies, one Grenadier company, and a 'Flanquer' company of light infantry. The uniforms of the 2nd Regiment were only slightly modified from those in use under the Confederation of the Rhine, and even in the 1st Regiment many wore the old costume, even though the new uniform had officially been issued.

The sergeant of the 2nd Regiment illustrated in Plate 42 shows the old-style uniform (which was worn until 1820). The shako was covered in black waterproof material, covering the brass plate. Pompoms were in the company colours: light blue for the first company, white for the second, yellow for the third, and green for the fourth. The Grenadiers wore a busby (see Plate 44) and the 'Flanquer' company green cords and yellow-tipped green plume on the shako; they were further distinguished by green epaulettes with yellow 'crescents', and yellow sword-knots. 'Flanquers' bore yellow hunting-horns on their turnbacks. Also of note were the yellow-buff belts, peculiar to the Nassau regiments.

Though not re-uniformed, the 2nd Regiment had been reorganised in 1814, each battalion to consist of a Grenadier, 'Flanquer', three Fusilier and one Rifle company; they were issued with British muskets at the same time.

43. Netherlands: Flanquer, 1st Nassau Regiment. Officer, 1st Nassau Regiment

Plate 43 illustrates the new uniform of the 1st Nassau Regiment, though some still retained the older style. The shakos and cartridge-pouches of this regiment were covered with white linen. Shako-plates were like that shown on the officers' shako in this illustration, though the 'Flanquers' had badges in the shape of hunting-horns, with the regimental number inside the curl. Pompoms were in company colours, being yellow for the first, white for the second, light blue for the third, and black for the fourth. The 'Flanquers' had yellow shako-cords and yellow-tipped green plumes. The rank and file of the Fusilier companies wore black shoulder-straps edged yellow. Officially, white linen trousers were authorised for summer wear. Equipment was French style, with the distinctive yellow-buff belts; cartridge-pouches were black leather, and bore a brass grenade for the Grenadier Company, and a hunting-horn for the 'Flanquers'.

44. Netherlands: Grenadier, 2nd Nassau Regiment. Grenadier, 1st Nassau Regiment

Plate 44 shows the two variations of the Nassau Grenadier uniform, the 1st Regiment wearing the new style, and the 2nd the old. Both regiments wore the busby, though on campaign the ornaments were stripped off; officers' busbies were similar, but with gold cords. The 1st Regiment's Grenadiers wore red shoulder-rolls, but those of the 2nd retained the red epalettes. Grenadiers' turnback-badges consisted of yellow grenades. The sword-knots were of the distinctive red colour.

The Nassau troops in the Waterloo campaign were organised as follows:

2nd Netherlands Division: three battalions, 2nd Nassau Regiment; 1st and 3rd Battalions, Regiment of Orange Nassau.

Nassau Contingent (General von Kruse): three battalions, 1st Nassau Regiment.

The combined total strength was 7,180.

45. France – Napoleon.

Rising from total obscurity to control the largest European empire since that of Rome, Napoleon Bonaparte was the most outstanding in an age of outstanding characters. His achievements, by brilliant generalship and an incredible personal magnetism, are unrivalled in history.

By 1815, Napoleon was no longer the man who had conquered Europe; afflicted by an assortment of illnesses and wearied by years of campaigning, he was unable to conduct his campaigns in the manner which had brought him victory on a score of fields. After the

final burst of energy in the campaigns of 1814, all else was downhill. Nevertheless, he was still the most feared commander in Europe, and it required the presence of Britain's greatest general and the unwavering courage of Blücher to bring about his final defeat.

Plate 45 shows Napoleon as he probably appeared at Waterloo, in the familiar and now legendary grey greatcoat and plain cocked hat, on the famous white arab, 'Marengo', named after one of the Emperor's victories in a happier age.

46. France: Trooper, Horse Grenadiers of the Imperial Guard.
Officer, Dragoons of the Imperial Guard

The Imperial Guard, the now-legendary bodyguard of the Emperor, consisted of all branches of cavalry, artillery and infantry; it was in effect an army within an army, composed of the élite, though, like the remainder of the French Army, was ill-equipped and under-strength when compared to its heyday. As was customary, however, the Guard was provided for before the line, and consequently their dress perhaps reflected decayed splendour rather than the somewhat ragged appearance of the remainder of the French Army.

The Guard Dragoons and Horse Grenadiers were brigaded together under Lt.-Gen. Count Guyot, a total of thirteen squadrons with a strength of

1,519. General Jamin commanded the Horse Grenadiers, but the old commander of the Dragoons, Ornano, had been wounded in a duel and was unfit, so General Letort was their commanding officer during the Waterloo campaign.

The Dragoons wore a uniform but little modified from their full dress, including the impressive and decorative helmet, but the Horse Grenadiers were but a shadow of their former magnificence. The bearskin caps were stripped of ornaments, and most wore the plain, single-breasted 'surtout', though some were compelled to appear in a variety of forage-caps and hats. The trumpeters still endeavoured to reflect their former glory, wearing white bearskin bonnets and sky-blue coats. Horse-furniture was of a similar style for both corps, consisting of the square-cut shabraque, with holster-covers, the Dragoon colour being green and the Horse Grenadier blue, both with orange lace; officers, of course, retained the more ornate, gold-laced housings.

47. France: Officer, Polish squadron, Imperial Guard Lancer Regiment. Trooper, 'Red' squadron, Imperial Guard Lancer Regiment

There had been three regiments of Lancers in the Imperial Guard, but in the Waterloo campaign there was but one, a 'composite' unit formed from the old Polish Lancers (who wore blue uniforms) and the Dutch Lancers (uniformed in red). Both sections retained their old uniforms, though modified for campaign; the czapkas or 'lancer-caps' were covered with 'waterproofs', the lapels of the 'kurtka' or lancer-jacket (in many cases) reversed so that the facing colour showed only as a thin piping around the lapels, the service overalls were adopted, and the lance-pennons enclosed in waterproof cases. Some British eye-witness accounts of the campaign report that the trumpeters and some of the officers of the Polish squadron wore their white full-dress uniforms with crimson facings, but this must be considered extremely unlikely; in all probability the trumpeters wore sky-blue uniforms with crimson facings and piping, and officers the usual service dress. One officer, however, wore the magnificent uniform of the old 'Red' Lancers, General Edouard de Colbert, their old commander, who charged at Waterloo in gold-laced scarlet kurtka and overalls, made even more striking by the addition of the distinguishing features of his rank. He charged on 18 June with his left arm in a sling, having been wounded at Quatre Bras — such was the devotion to duty and heroism which infected every member of the Imperial Guard.

The Combined Lancer Regiment was brigaded with the Chasseurs à Cheval of the Imperial Guard under Lt.-Gen. Lefebvre-Desnoëttes, giving a total of nineteen squadrons, 1,971 men. In May (though the strength had declined by the time of the battle), the Lancers mustered 964 of all ranks; the regiment's two commandants were Colonel du Bois de la Ferrière and Baron Jerzmanowski, though the former was left at the regimental depot because of suspected Royalist sympathies. The 1st Squadron was composed of the old Polish Lancers (who had followed Napoleon to Elba); the remainder came from the Royal Guard (as the Imperial Guard became after the Bourbon Restoration), ex-'Red' Lancers from retirement, and a few recruits from the line.

48. France: Officer, Chasseurs à Cheval of the Imperial Guard.
Trooper, Elite Gendarmes of the Imperial Guard

The Chasseurs à Cheval of the Imperial Guard, traditionally the Emperor's closest bodyguard, wore a uniform little changed from the greatest days of the Empire. Exactly which uniform was worn at Waterloo, however (as in many other cases) is something of a mystery; either the dolman, worn without the pelisse (as illustrated), or possibly the 'petite tenue', consisting of a dark green tail-coat and red waistcoat, were worn; in all probability, varying combinations of the two would be the actual dress at Waterloo, with either overalls (as illustrated) or dark green breeches. Lace of the rank and file was orange. The busbies (known in the French Army as 'colpacks') were stripped of their plumes, bag and cords for the campaign.

It has been estimated that about 500 were uniformed in the dolman and overalls, the remainder wearing the other dress; but there is no conclusive evidence. Trumpeters probably wore similar busbies, sky-blue dolmans with crimson facings and mixed crimson and gold braid, and sky-blue overalls with a crimson stripe down the outer seam. Horse-furniture was of a similar pattern for all ranks to that illustrated in Plate 48, though the troopers' shabraques were laced in orange; those of the trumpeters were sky-blue, laced orange and piped red. The service dress sabretache is illustrated; those of the rank and file were also black leather, but bearing large brass badges of the crowned Imperial eagle.

The Elite Gendarmes, another 'heavy' branch of the Guard cavalry, wore their bearskins devoid of the normal decorations, and almost certainly had the 'surtout' coat, though, as in all sections of the French Army, there was considerable 'non-uniformity'; on 1 June they were described as wearing 'the most uniform dress possible', a phrase which illustrates their poor condition.

On 24 April a squadron of 'Mamelukes' was officially attached to the Chasseurs à Cheval, but whether it ever materialised is another matter, and if it did there is no evidence to show that the elaborate Oriental dress worn prior to 1814 was adopted; certainly many items of this nature were ordered, 'kaouks' (Oriental head-dress), special braid, etc., and according to the quartermaster's register, some of these items were actually issued, but whether they were used, and whether the mameluke squadron marched as a unit in 1815, is one of the minor mysteries surrounding the campaign.

In May 1815, the Chasseurs à Cheval, commanded by Commandant Lallemand, mustered 1,267 of all ranks; they formed part of Lefebvre-Desnoëttes' brigade with the Guard Lancers. At the time of the battle, the Elite Gendarmes had a strength of only 102 men.

49. France: Private, Grenadiers of the Imperial Guard.
Officer, Grenadiers of the Imperial Guard

The Grenadiers of the Imperial Guard have undoubtedly become the most famous corps of all those engaged in the Napoleonic Wars. They have been surrounded by a mystique, the epitome of loyalty, bravery, experience and invincibility. There were four regiments of Grenadiers at Waterloo, a shadow of their former self.

The 1st Grenadiers, under General Petit, were the élite of the French Army. One thousand strong, a third were veterans of between twenty and twenty-five campaigns; four-fifths wore the Legion of Honour. They were uniformed as in Plate 49, with their bearskin bonnets devoid of ornaments, in cross-belted greatcoats, and blue trousers; it is interesting to note that their cartridge pouches were covered with white canvas, with the design of the crowned eagle and four bursting grenades painted on in black. Officers generally wore the bicorn hat and 'surtout' coat.

The 2nd Grenadiers, · also 1,000 strong (or slightly more), were commanded by Baron Christiani, almost all dressed like the 1st Regiment, and, like the 1st, formed the veteran élite of the French Army.

The 3rd Grenadiers, raised on 8 April, were slightly stronger, and commanded by Poret de Morvan. Their uniform was also regulation, but with a more ragged appearance; there were few bearskin caps, a motley collection of shakos, hats and forage-caps taking their place; some wore incomplete equipment, and many musket-slings were replaced by string.

The 4th Grenadiers, raised on 9 May, under General Harlet, were perhaps the worst-uniformed corps in the campaign; it has been stated that scarcely twenty men were uniformed alike. Numbering only 500, the men had all been drafted from regiments of the line, and wore every variety of costume, some uniforms resembling those of the provincial national guard. The four regiments, numbering two battalions each except the 4th, which had only one, composed the Old Guard Division under Count Roguet.

Casualties at Waterloo were horrific; whole battalions were destroyed, men dying where they stood rather than retreat. The 4th Regiment was almost annihilated, Harlet and all the captains and lieutenants becoming casualties. But perhaps the most epic incident concerned the 2nd Battalion of the 3rd Grenadiers; when the French Army broke, the battalion stood its ground in square, repelling attack after attack, until artillery was brought up and fired at point-blank range at the square, which collapsed, the survivors forming a triangle, not giving an inch, and allowing some of the fugitives of the Allied pursuit a moment's respite. Attacked again, and reduced from 500 to less than 150, those still alive refused to surrender; firing a final volley, they flung themselves to destruction upon the sabres of the surrounding cavalry.

50. France: Chasseur, Chasseurs à Pied of the Imperial Guard. Sergeant, Chasseurs à Pied of the Imperial Guard

There were four regiments of Chasseurs à Pied of the Imperial Guard, of which the first two wore the uniform shown in Plate 50, consisting of the bearskin bonnet, without ornaments, the greatcoat, and the blue overall trousers. Under the greatcoat was worn the regulation coat and white waistcoat. Officers generally wore a uniform akin to that shown in the previous plate, consisting of a bicorn hat and 'surtout', often with the greatcoat rolled over the shoulder as an added protection against swordslashes. Of the Old Guard, only the 1st Grenadiers and the 1st Chasseurs carried 'Eagles'; however, small company

flags were carried like that illustrated. Epaulettes should have been worn on the greatcoat, but it is likely that, because of the shortage of equipment, this fashion was not universal. Some men carried their bicorn hats strapped to the rear of the knapsack, covered in striped blue canvas.

The 1st Chasseurs included a few veterans, mostly among the N.C.O.s, though most had entered the Guard in 1813, and the regiment was made up to its strength of 1,307 men and forty-one officers on 1 June by drafting in light infantrymen from the line. The regiment was commanded by Cambronne.

The 2nd Chasseurs, under Pelet, consisted of thirty-five officers and 1,200 men (1 June), and also included a number of veterans.

The 3rd Chasseurs, under Colonel Malet, with thirty-eight officers and 1,100 men, and the 4th Chasseurs, under General Henrion, which had only one battalion (the other regiments each having two) were, like the 4th Grenadiers, dressed in an odd assortment of every conceivable style and pattern. The four regiments formed General Michel's 2nd Old Guard Division.

Casualties, like those of the Grenadiers, were appalling. Twenty-five out of the thirty officers of the 3rd Chasseurs present at Waterloo fell; all the 4th's officers were down when the remnants of the battalion joined up with the 3rd. One battalion of the 2nd Regiment was the last Guard unit to disperse, retiring in good order to La Belle Alliance; the other battalion of the 2nd, with Pelet, held on in Plancenoit until the end. Gathering after the battle, the 1st Chasseurs formed the rearguard of the retiring French Army.

51. France: Officer, Voltigeurs of the Imperial Guard. Private, Tirailleurs of the Imperial Guard

The Tirailleurs and Voltigeurs of the Imperial Guard constituted part of the 'Young Guard'. The uniform of both corps was similar, consisting of the 'habit veste', the Tirailleurs being distinguished by red pompoms on the shakos, red facings, and white eagle badges on the turnbacks. The Voltigeurs wore the same uniform, but with green pompoms (gold for officers), yellow collars, and green eagles on the turnbacks. Epaulettes were red for the Tirailleurs, and green with yellow 'crescents' for the Voltigeurs. Officers wore gold lace; some shakos were covered with a 'waterproof' as shown in this plate. Both corps carried an interesting variation on the standard equipment: only N.C.O.s were armed with the short sabre, so privates wore only one cross-belt, the bayonet-scabbard being attached to that. However, there were some dressed in non-regulation styles.

The 1st Division of the Young Guard, commanded by General Barrois, comprised the 1st and 3rd Tirailleurs and 1st and 3rd Voltigeurs. Each regiment numbered approximately 1,000 men, though the 1st Voltigeurs had

nearer 1,200. The Young Guard suffered heavy casualties in the defence of Plancenoit, but could not hold the position, and a battalion of the 2nd Chasseurs à Pied were sent to assist; they arrived to find Colonel Hurel of the 3rd Voltigeurs running after his retreating troops in an attempt to rally them. Forming behind the Chasseurs, the Young Guard returned to the fight and held on until nightfall, until the decimated French finally gave way, leaving Pelet with a handful of his Chasseurs still defying the Prussians.

52. France: Officer, Horse Artillery, Imperial Guard. Gunner, Foot Artillery, Imperial Guard

The Imperial Guard included both Horse and Foot Artillery batteries; though the Horse batteries were reasonably complete, there had been great difficulty experienced in forming and equipping the Foot batteries prior to the campaign.

The Horse Artillery wore their distinctive Hussar-style uniform, with variations brought about by shortage of equipment and the rigours of campaigning. The busbies were worn without ornaments, and either the coat and waistcoat as illustrated, or the braided dolman. Uniforms of the rank and file had red braid and ornaments, to replace the more ornate officers' version illustrated in Plate 52; overalls were worn by the majority, these being dark blue with black leather strapping and a red stripe down the outer seam of each leg. Shabraques of the other ranks were similar in design to that illustrated, but with red lace. Belts were of white leather; the service dress sabretache was of black leather, and bore a brass badge of the crowned Imperial eagle over crossed cannon-barrels. Trumpeters wore busbies with light blue bags, light blue coats with dark blue lapels, collars and cuffs, crimson piping and yellow lace; their overalls were like those of the other ranks, but shabraques were light blue, with red lace.

The Foot Artillery wore the peaked bearskin cap, with all the ornaments removed. Greatcoats were worn, these being of a shade known as 'steel blue', a mixture of blue and white threads; the greatcoats were distinguished by the red collar-patch. The regulation equipment was worn, with the cartridge-pouch covered with a black 'waterproof'.

The Guard Artillery Train wore shakos, steel-grey single-breasted jackets with dark blue collars and cuffs, and red piping; grey breeches were worn with high riding-boots. These troops were responsible for the transportation of supplies and ammunition.

There were nine Foot batteries and four Horse batteries attached to the Imperial Guard, under the overall command of Lt.-Gen. Desvaux de St. Maurice, who was killed by an exploding shell at about 3.30 p.m. on 18 June; command passed to Lallemand, commander of the Foot Artillery, who was himself wounded later in the day.

53. France: Private, Marines of the Imperial Guard. Officer, Engineers of the Imperial Guard

The Marines of the Imperial Guard, numbering about 104, did not wear their famous, elaborately-laced uniforms, but instead clothing of great simplicity; waist-length jackets known as 'caracots' with orange lacing and brass shoulder-scales, and dark blue overalls. Their shakos were covered in black 'waterproofs', and they were armed with dragoon muskets.

The Marines, dressed 'as well as possible under the circumstances', still retained some of their own distinctive features of equipment, with their black belts with brass regimental plates, and the unique design of sabre. Officers were officially supposed to wear naval uniform, though on campaign their dress consisted of a bicorn hat, a single-breasted blue 'surtout' coat with gold lace, blue or white waistcoat, and blue trousers. Like the other ranks, officers wore black leather equipment.

The Engineers of the Imperial Guard, about 109 strong, may have worn the famous black-crested helmet of Carabinier style, or the standard pattern shako instead; there is no real evidence one way or the other. The uniforms were basically of the same cut as those of the Imperial Guard Grenadiers, being dark blue with black collar, cuffs and lapels, all piped scarlet, with scarlet turnbacks and epaulettes. In working dress ('tenue de travail'), the dark blue forage-cap or 'bonnet de police' was worn in conjunction with a long-sleeved blue waistcoat and blue trousers. Officers, however, on campaign wore the uniform illustrated, comprising the single-breasted 'surtout' and bicorn. Equipment was identical to that of the Grenadiers, but with very minor differences, notably black bayonet-scabbards and steel fittings to the muskets.

54. France: Officer, 1st Cuirassiers. Trooper, 11th Cuirassiers

The armoured cuirassiers have become the symbol of the French cavalry in general; their magnificent courage in repeatedly charging the British squares caught the imagination of all who witnessed the battle. The cuirassiers, the supreme 'shock weapon' of the French Army, failed to break the Allied line, and caused their own destruction in so doing.

The uniform depicted on the mounted figure was that common to most of the cuirassier regiments at Waterloo, with certain varying features. The plume was worn on campaign by officers only, if at all. The cloth edging or 'cuffs' on the cuirass was of red, edged white, for the rank and file, their helmets and cuirasses being much less ornate than those of the officers. The buff breeches were sometimes replaced by brown, and often by grey overalls, with or without black leather strapping. Other ranks wore white leather belts. Shabraques of the rank and file were similar to those of the officers, but laced in white, with white sheepskins edged with the facing colour. Trumpeters' sheepskins were black.

The jackets of the rank and file had red epaulettes, and were distinguished by the facing colour on the collar, cuffs, turnbacks and cuff-flaps; turnbacks bore blue grenade badges. The facings of the twelve regiments present at Waterloo were as follows:

Regiment	Collar, turnbacks	Cuffs	Cuff-flaps
1st	Red	Red	Red
2nd	Red	Red	Blue
3rd	Red	Blue	Red
4th	Light orange	Light orange	Light orange
5th	Light orange	Light orange	Blue
6th	Light orange	Blue	Light orange
7th	Yellow	Yellow	Yellow
8th	Yellow	Yellow	Blue
9th	Yellow	Blue	Yellow
10th	Rose	Rose	Rose
11th	Rose	Rose	Blue
12th	Rose	Blue	Rose

However, there is evidence to show that the 11th Regiment did not have cuirasses in the campaign, wearing instead single-breasted blue 'surtouts' with piping of the facing colour, as illustrated in Plate 54.

Trumpeters generally wore helmets with white horsehair manes and aigrettes, and either green 'surtouts' with regimental facings and Imperial lace (yellow with a green embroidered design), or blue jackets with white lace.

How effective the cuirasses were is doubtful; certainly they were a good protection against bayonet and sword, but would not stop a musket-ball; eyewitnesses of the French charges compared the sound made by the musket-balls piercing cuirasses to hailstones falling on a roof. The extra weight of their heavy armour was a disadvantage at times; Wellington himself remarked that 'Those that were not killed were so encumbered by their cuirasses and jackboots that they could not get up, but

lay sprawling and kicking like so many turned turtles'. Both British and Dutch armies adopted the cuirass after Waterloo, not so much because of utility as to commemorate the wonderful valour and magnificent appearance of some of the finest cavalry in the world.

55. France: Trooper, 2nd Dragoons. Officer, 7th Dragoons

The thirteen regiments of Dragoons present in the Waterloo campaign wore the same basic uniform, though with numerous variations. The brass helmets were worn without plumes on campaign; officers' turbans were of leopard-skin, those of the other ranks being brown fur. The dark green jackets had lapels, turnbacks, collar, cuffs and cuff-flaps in the facing colours, and the shoulder-straps were piped in the facing. The turnbacks were ornamented with green grenade badges. Officers some-

Regiment	Lapels, turnbacks	Collar	Cuffs	Cuff-flaps
2nd	Scarlet	Green	Scarlet	Green
4th	Scarlet	Scarlet	Scarlet	Scarlet
5th	Scarlet	Green	Scarlet	Green
6th	Scarlet	Scarlet	Green	Scarlet
7th	Carmine	Carmine	Carmine	Carmine
11th	Carmine	Green	Carmine	Green
12th	Carmine	Carmine	Green	Carmine
13th	Rose	Rose	Rose	Rose
14th	Rose	Green	Rose	Rose
15th	Rose	Rose	Green	Rose
16th	Rose	Rose	Rose	Rose
17th	Rose	Green	Rose	Green
20th	Yellow	Green	Yellow	Green

times wore the 'surtout' coat as illustrated, with silver epaulettes and silver grenades in the turnbacks. Horse-furniture was shaped like that of the cuirassiers, but of dark green with white lace, and white sheepskins edged with the facing colour; trumpeters' sheepskins were black. Officers' shabraques were without sheepskins, and were laced silver.

Facing colours for the regiments engaged in the Waterloo campaign were as shown in the previous table.

Trumpeters generally wore helmets with white horsehair manes and aigrettes, with green jackets faced with the regimental colour, decorated with 'Imperial' lace, with red epaulettes; but there were many variations on the regulation style, as indeed there were for the uniforms of the officers and other ranks; some sources, for example, show the 20th Dragoons with black leather equipment.

56/57. France: Trooper, Elite Company, 6th Chevau-Léger-Lanciers. Officer, 6th Chevau-Léger-Lanciers. Brigadier, Elite Company, 1st Chasseurs à Cheval. Trooper, 6th Chasseurs à Cheval. Officer, Elite Company, 6th Chasseurs à Cheval

All six French regiments of Chevau-Léger-Lanciers were present in the Waterloo campaign. They wore brass helmets, with fur turbans (leopardskin for officers), with black crests; the Elite Company of the 6th Regiment (corresponding to Grenadiers in the infantry) had helmet-crests of red wool. Green jackets were worn with distinctive facing colours on the collar, cuffs, lapels and turnbacks, the latter bearing a crowned 'N' in green. In some cases, however, the lapels were turned in to show only a narrow piping of the facing colour around the edge. Elite companies wore red epaulettes, the remainder having green shoulder-straps piped in the regimental facing. Leather equipment was white, except for the 6th, which wore ochre belts and gauntlets. Officers were distinguished by gold lace and epaulettes. Overalls were dark green with black leather strapping, with a stripe of the facing colour down the outer seam; one exception was the officers of the 6th, who wore madder-red overalls.

Officers' shabraques were dark green, shaped like those of the Chasseurs à Cheval, with gold lace edging; the rank and file had white sheepskins, trimmed with the regimental facing colour. Valises were also dark green, edged with gold for officers and yellow for other ranks. Trumpeters had black sheepskins. Generally, Trumpeters wore the 'Imperial Livery', green with 'Imperial' lace, though there is evidence to show that those of the Elite companies of the 1st and 2nd Regiments wore dark blue coats with regimental facings, with the addition of white lace and epaulettes. Trumpeters' helmet-crests were white. The regulation pattern lance was carried, with black leather hand-grips (ochre for the 6th Regiment), and red over white pennons, though on campaign these were often covered with a black 'waterproof' case. Regimental facing-colours were as follows: 1st Regiment, scarlet; 2nd, light orange; 3rd, rose; 4th, crimson; 5th, sky-blue; 6th, red.

The Chasseurs à Cheval were another branch of light cavalry; nine regiments were present in the Waterloo campaign. There is some doubt as to the head-dress worn by the 1st Regiment, but it is likely that it was the crested helmet as illustrated, originally adopted after the Bourbon Restoration, with the scroll on the helmet reading 'Chasseurs du Roi'. Before the 1815 campaign began, this scroll was hammered to read 'Chasseurs du i', the 'i' standing for 'Empereur'. Other regiments wore the standard pattern shako, often covered with a black 'waterproof', though some officers wore cylindrical Hussar-style head-dress. In addition, some N.C.O.s and members of Elite companies, as well as a large number of officers, continued to wear the fur busby.

The dark green double-breasted jacket was worn by all ranks, though the single-breasted 'surtout' was also worn; the jacket was trimmed with the regimental facing colour on the collar, cuffs and turnbacks; and was also piped in the regimental facing. Overalls were dark green, with black leather strapping, and stripes of the regimental facing colour down the outer seams; however, some dark grey overalls were worn. Officers wore silver epaulettes. Elite companies were distinguished by red epaulettes, the remainder having green shoulder-straps piped in the regimental facing colour. The turnbacks were ornamented with green grenade badges.

Shabraques for the officers were green, edged with silver lace; the rank and file had white sheepskins, edged with the regimental facing; some trumpeters had black sheepskins.

The facing colours of the regiments present in the campaign were as follows:

Regiment	Collar	Collar-piping	Cuffs, turnbacks
1st	Scarlet	Green	Scarlet
3rd	Scarlet	Green	Scarlet
4th	Yellow	Green	Yellow
6th	Yellow	Green	Yellow
7th	Pink	Green	Pink
8th	Green	Pink	Pink
9th	Pink	Green	Pink
11th	Green	Crimson	Crimson
12th	Crimson	Green	Crimson

It should be noted that there were regimental variations to the collar piping; the rule that the collars of the facing colour were piped green, and that green collars were piped with the facing colour, did not always apply.

58. France: Officer, 1st Carabiniers. Trooper, 2nd Carabiniers

The two regiments of Carabiniers formed part of the heavy cavalry, being uniformed in a style similar to the Cuirassiers. Their helmets and cuirasses, however, were of brass (copper for officers). The white uniform, adopted in 1810, had sky-blue collars and turn-backs for both regiments, the only distinguishing feature being the cuffs, which were red with white piping for the 1st Regiment, with white cuff-flaps piped sky-blue; and sky-blue with white piping for the 2nd Regiment, with sky-blue flaps piped white.

Breeches were replaced by overalls on campaign, these being of dark grey or 'drab'. Belts were similar to those worn by the Elite Gendarmes of the Imperial Guard, being ochre with white edges. Officers' shabraques were also sky-blue, but without sheepskins; they were laced with a double silver band, and bore silver grenade badges in the rear corners; holster-caps were often covered in black fur.

Both regiments of Carabiniers formed part of Lt.-Gen. Roussel d'Hurbal's 12th Cavalry Division of Kellerman's 3rd Corps.

59. France: Trooper, Elite Company, 1st Hussars. Officer, 4th Hussars

Only five regiments of Hussars were present in the Waterloo campaign. Their uniform, traditionally the most flamboyant of the French Army, consisted of the cylindrical shako adopted in 1813–14 (though some may have retained the older pattern, and some Elite companies the busby), the characteristic braided dolman or tail-less jacket, and the fur-edged pelisse, normally worn hanging from one shoulder. On campaign, however, the pelisse was almost invariably worn as a jacket, over the dolman, or discarded entirely. With this uniform, overalls were worn, either of grey or distinctive regimental colours. The Elite companies were distinguished by red plumes on the occasions when plumes were worn in the field.

As with most of the more decorative parts of the uniform, the laced full dress sabretache was usually replaced by a more utilitarian model, of plain black leather bearing a metal badge, usually the regimental number. Pelisses were edged with black or dark brown fur for all the regiments engaged in the campaign. Officers were distinguished by 'metal' lace (i.e. either gold or silver, depending whether the rank and file wore yellow or white braid), laced belts, and more ornate shakos. The various colourings for the regiments concerned are listed below :

Regt.	Shako	Dolman	Pelisse	Collar	Cuffs	Overalls	Lace	Sash
1st	Black	Sky-blue	Sky-blue	Sky-blue	Red	Sky-blue	White	Red/White
4th	Red	Blue	Red	Blue	Red	Blue	Yellow	Red/Yellow
5th	Red	Sky-blue	White	Sky-blue	White	Sky-blue	Yellow	Red/Yellow
6th	Red	Red	Blue	Red	Red	Blue	Yellow	Red/Yellow
7th	Light Green	Green	Green	Red	Red	Green	Yellow	Red/Yellow

Note: the 'Blue' of the 4th and 6th Regiments was a royal blue shade; the yellow lace of the 4th had a thin blue line woven in.

Officers' shabraques were shaped like those of the Chasseurs à Cheval, usually of the same colour as the dolman, with silver or gold lace; troopers had white sheepskins edged with a 'wolf's tooth' design in red (sky-blue for the 5th Regiment).

60. France: Officer, Foot Artillery. Private, Horse Artillery

The Horse Artillery of the Line wore uniforms much simpler than those of the Guard units; the uniform shown in this plate is that worn on campaign. Officers, however, often wore Hussar-style uniforms on service, of dark blue with scarlet cuffs, and gold braid and lacing. The pelisse was also dark blue, laced gold, with grey or fawn fur; with this uniform, a fur busby with red bag was worn. On campaign, however, a long-tailed dark blue coat was often worn, or (more commonly in 1815) a short-tailed jacket like that of the other ranks, both with scarlet cuffs and gold epaulettes; shakos, minus their cords and plumes, were often worn in the field. Either dark blue or grey overalls or breeches were worn. The sabretache was carried when the dolman or pelisse was worn, having a dark blue face with gold lace edging and devices, the latter varying with the individual artillery regiment.

The rank and file of the Foot Artillery wore uniforms of a similar style to that of the officer illustrated, but with red epaulettes or dark blue shoulder-straps piped red, with dark blue breeches and black gaiters, or dark blue trousers. Shakos had red pompoms, and (very occasionally by 1815) red lace. The equipment carried was of the standard pattern; gunners were armed with muskets and short sabres.

The Artillery Train of the Line, like that of the Guard, wore steel-grey uniforms with dark blue collar, lapels, cuffs and turnbacks, with steel-grey shoulder-straps, piped blue. On campaign, they wore shakos covered with black oilskin, and overalls were either grey, 'drab', or dark brown, often with leather strapping. Officers wore silver epaulettes, light cavalry belts and sabres, and red leather pouch-belts with silver edging. The 'Train des Equipages', or Equipment Train, wore uniforms of a similar design, but with brown facings.

The Artillery of the French Army was disposed in the following manner:

1st Army Corps: five Foot and one Horse battery: 46 guns.

2nd Army Corps: five Foot and one Horse battery: 46 guns.

3rd Army Corps: four Foot and one Horse battery: 38 guns.

4th Army Corps: four Foot and one Horse battery: 38 guns.

5th Army Corps: four Foot and one Horse battery: 38 guns.

Reserve Cavalry: eight Horse batteries: 48 guns.

61. France: Grenadier Officer, Line Infantry. Eagle-bearer, 45th Regiment

Infantry officers, unlike some of the rank and file, were uniformed in the regulation style, wearing either the double-breasted 'habit veste' or the single-breasted 'surtout'. The former had white lapels and red facings; the latter was often plain blue. Epaulettes were of gold lace. Turnbacks bore badges of the crowned letter 'N', with grenades for Grenadiers and horns for Voltigeurs (these were scarlet and yellow respectively for other ranks), in

gold for officers. After the Bourbon Restoration, however, some regiments had had the Imperial devices replaced by Royalist emblems, which were hastily removed upon Napoleon's return, and no time was available to replace the Imperial badges.

Officers' shakos were gold-laced, but the majority were probably enclosed in cloth or oilskin covers on campaign. The small red ribbon on the breast of the Grenadier officer's 'surtout' is that of the Legion of Honour. All manner of legwear was worn; trousers of blue or grey, or breeches and knee-boots. The gorget (the symbol of commissioned rank hung around the neck, a memorial of the neck-guard of a suit of armour) was worn even on campaign. Many officers carried water-gourds and other assorted items of equipment; straight-bladed swords were carried by the 'centre' companies, and curved sabres by the Grenadiers and Voltigeurs (though there were exceptions to this regulation).

The 'Eagle' was the most precious possession of the regiment; it was a wooden pole, with a large gilt Imperial eagle attached. Of secondary importance was the flag attached to the pole; on occasion, the pole alone was carried. On campaign, when the flag was attached, it was carried furled around the pole, covered in a waterproof 'case', being unfurled before the regiment went into action. In battle, the 'Eagle' served as a rallying-point, symbolising the loyalty between troops and Emperor. The 'Eagle' of the regiment illustrated, the

45th Line, was captured when the regiment was ridden down by the British 'Union' Brigade; Sergeant Charles Ewart of the 2nd (Royal North British) Dragoons has left a classic account of how he captured the standard, which shows how desperately the Eagle-escort fought to retain their flag, Ewart being compelled to kill three before he took possession of his trophy. The 105th Regiment also lost their 'Eagle' at Waterloo; Ewart and Corporal Francis Stiles of the 1st Dragoons were both commissioned for their bravery.

62. France: Fusilier, 1st Line Infantry.
Grenadier Sergeant, 72nd Line Infantry

Some of the French infantry were very poorly equipped; indeed, it has been suggested that some of the conscripts were issued only a shako, greatcoat, belts and musket, wearing their civilian clothes underneath.

French regiments comprised the 'centre' or Fusilier companies, distinguished by dark blue shoulder-straps piped red, the élite Grenadiers, who wore red epaulettes, and the 'Voltigeurs' or light infantry who wore epaulettes in various combinations of yellow and green. Those companies with epaulettes wore them on the greatcoat as well as on the 'habit-veste'. Shakos were of the regulation infantry pattern, though those of some Grenadiers were ornamented with red lace.

Plumes or pompoms were red for Grenadiers, yellow and/or green for Voltigeurs, and in 'company colours' for Fusiliers, either dark green, sky-blue, yellow or violet, the 1st Battalion of each regiment having pompoms of solid colour, those of the other battalions being white discs edged in the company distinctive. Shako-plates consisted of the Imperial eagle on a semi-circular shield, bearing the regimental number. However, there is evidence to show that some regiments, after the Bourbon Restoration, converted their shako-plates into Royalist ones by cutting off the eagle, leaving just the shield part; there was insufficient time after Napoleon's return to replace these with whole 'Imperial' plates, and, as illustrated for the 1st Regiment, the half-plates continued in use.

A great variety of legwear was used, breeches and gaiters, or various types of overall being the most common, in a wide range of colours, sometimes tied around the ankle with string. Greatcoats were either grey, 'drab', or brown. The standard infantry equipment was used, though many men lacked some items. Cartridge-pouches were frequently covered with white canvas. The roll on top of the hide knapsack was sometimes enclosed in a blue and white striped cover.

The uniform worn by drummers presents another minor problem. The old 'Imperial Livery', of green with 'Imperial' lace, had in many cases been replaced; in others, the lace had been removed. There are reports that, upon

Napoleon's return, having no time to replace the lace, the green coats were daubed with yellow paint as a hasty substitute. However, some drummers wore a blue uniform like the other ranks; a picture of the 1st Regiment shows this worn with white lace and epaulettes, while one of the 2nd shows a drummer in a blue coat with red collar, cuffs and lapels, all profusely laced with orange.

63. France: Voltigeur Officer, Light Infantry. Voltigeur, 1st Light Infantry

The French Light Infantry wore uniforms of the same basic pattern as the infantry, but with their own distinctions; lapels were dark blue. The Light Infantry contained three branches: Chasseur companies, distinguished by red collars, green epaulettes with red 'crescents', and green shako-plumes; Carabinier companies (corresponding to Grenadiers in the Line), distinguished by red collars and epaulettes, and red shako-plumes; and Voltigeurs, who wore yellow collars and epaulettes of various mixtures of red, green and yellow. However, more often than not these basic rules varied from regiment to regiment, the colouring being more or less standardised to red for Carabiniers and red and yellow for Voltigeurs, these colours being combined with the green of the Chasseurs. Turnback-badges consisted of crowned 'N' devices for Chasseurs, grenades or combined grenades and hunting-horns for Carabiniers, and hunting-horns for Voltigeurs. Officers were distinguished by silver lace and epaulettes.

On campaign, shakos were frequently covered with cloth of various colours, which concealed the white metal plates and coloured lace worn by some regiments. Greatcoats, when worn, were of the standard pattern, with the epaulettes worn outside. Trousers were generally blue, though the shortages of the time resulted in a large variety of colours and styles; the blue trousers were often laced yellow (silver for officers). Equipment was of the standard pattern, the cartridge-pouches often being covered with white linen or canvas. Sabre-knots were in distinctive company colours, being red for Carabiniers, green with yellow or yellow with red tassels for Voltigeurs, and green or green and red for Chasseurs, though again there were many variations. Fatigue caps, or 'bonnets de police', were normally carried rolled underneath the cartridge pouch: they were blue, with tassels of the company distinctive colours. Light Infantry gorgets were of silver with gilt devices.

64. France: Fusilier, 2nd Swiss Regiment. Grenadier Officer, 2nd Swiss Regiment

The exact uniform and composition of this regiment during the Waterloo campaign is in doubt. Before Napoleon's

Abdication in 1814, his Swiss regiments consistently proved themselves to be among the finest in Europe. In 1815, however, many of the Swiss remained loyal to the King, in whose service they had been engaged, and only one battalion of about 730 men returned to the Emperor's service. This battalion was entitled the 'Deuxième Régiment Suisse', but whether it bore any relation to the previous 2nd Swiss Regiment is doubtful; perhaps Swiss volunteers were built up upon a cadre of the previous corps, but it is probably more likely that the battalion was entirely newly-raised. Brigaded in the 10th Infantry Division of Vandamme's III Corps, the Swiss regiment, true to the valour and magnificent courage of its predecessors, was almost completely wiped out in the attack on the bridge at Wavre.

The minor details of the uniform are a little in doubt, though in all probability the costume resembled that illustrated in Plate 64, being basically of the standard infantry cut, but in the traditional Swiss red colour, with dark blue facings and white piping, and gold epaulettes for officers.

65. Prussia: Adjutant-Offizier. Generalfeldmarschal Blücher

Generalfeldmarschal Gebhardt-Lebrecht v. Blücher, though seventy-two years of age at the time of Waterloo, and generally lacking in the tactical and strategic knowledge normally required to command an army, was genuinely lion-hearted and won his victories by perseverance rather than by tactical brilliance. His insistence to keep his word to march and link up with Wellington was a vital factor in the Allied victory: without 'Marshal Vorwärts' (as he was known to his men), the campaign could easily have had a different outcome.

The uniform worn by Blücher at Waterloo was in all probability the simple service dress worn by staff officers: the soft-topped cloth 'Schirmütze' cap, with simple grey greatcoat and cape, with the regulation Prussian sash of mixed silver and black threads.

The officer depicted in Plate 65 is an aide-de-camp, or 'Adjutant-Offizier'. This shows the uniform adopted in 1814, with the unique pattern of lacing on the coat or 'Kollet', with the bicorn hat normally worn in full dress.

On active service, general officers usually wore one of three versions of the staff uniform, worn with the red-piped grey Schirmütze and the standard grey trousers: either a double-breasted dark blue coat with scarlet facings and gold epaulettes, a single-breasted coat with gold-laced collar and cuffs with shoulder-straps of twisted silver braid, or the overcoat, usually coloured grey for generals of infantry and dark blue for generals of cavalry or artillery. However, there were exceptions: at Waterloo, for example, the commander of the IV Army Corps' Reserve Cavalry, Prince William of Prussia, wore the regimental uniform of the Brandenburg Dragoons.

66. Prussia : Trooper, 1st 'Koningin' Dragoons. Officer, 2nd (1st West Prussian) Dragoons

The Prussian Dragoon regiments wore the shako of standard pattern with the universal black waterproof cover for campaign dress. Although in full dress the Dragoons wore the 'Kollet' coat, on service the rank and file generally adopted the thigh-length 'Litewka' coat, this having the regimental facing colour on the collar, shoulder-straps and cuff-piping. Officers, however, often wore the 'leibrock', a garment not unlike the 'Kollet', on campaign as well as in full dress; the facing colour of this pattern was on the collar, cuffs and turnbacks. Officers' shoulder-straps were laced with the distinctions of their rank. The officer illustrated in Plate 66 is shown wearing the cloth cap or 'Feldmütze', which was of the Dragoon distinctive colour, light blue, with a band of the regimental facing colour. The standard grey overalls with black leather strapping were worn by all ranks. Shabraques were edged with a double line of the regimental facing colour.

The Dragoon regiments engaged in the Waterloo campaign wore the following facings and button-colours on their light blue uniforms:

Regiment	Facings	Buttons
1st 'Koningin' Regiment	Crimson	White
2nd (1st West Prussian) Regiment	White	White
5th (Brandenburg) Regiment	Black	Yellow
6th (Neumark) Regiment	Rose	White
7th (Rhenish) Regiment	White	Yellow

67. Prussia : Officer, 4th (1st Silesian) Hussars. Trooper, 6th (2nd Silesian) Hussars.

68. Prussia : Trumpeter, 3rd (Brandenburg) Hussars. Trooper, 9th (Rhenish) Hussars

Prussian Hussar uniform incorporated all the traditional features of that arm, in the braided dolman and pelisse. All regiments wore the shako, with the usual black cover, or occasionally a soft-topped cap, of grey cloth with a band of the dolman colour. Facing colours were borne on the collar and cuffs; pelisse-fur was white for troopers, black for N.C.O.s and grey for officers; on campaign, the pelisse was often worn as a jacket, over the dolman. Officers were distinguished by 'metal' (gold or silver) braid and buttons, depending on the colour (yellow or white) of the other ranks' braid. The standard grey overalls were worn by all ranks; the 'barrelled' sash was of two colours, these being the facing colour and the colour of the lace. Sabretaches were black leather for the two Silesian regiments, but of red cloth with yellow or white lace edging and 'F.W.' cipher for the other regiments. Officers wore laced shoulder-straps on both dolman and pelisse. Trumpeters, as usual in the Prussian Army, were distinguished by laced 'swallow's nest' wings worn on both dolman and pelisse. Cloaks, when worn, were white for the Brandenburg and Pommeranian Regiments, and grey for the remainder; their collars were in the colour of the dolman. On campaign, all ranks had black sheepskin shabraques, edged with a red 'wolf's teeth' design.

The distinguishing colours of the regiments in the Waterloo campaign are given below:

In 1808 infantry regiments were regulated to contain three battalions, one of Fusiliers and two of Musketeers; the old Grenadier companies, though still officially part of the regiment, were detached and formed into separate Grenadier battalions.

All regiments wore the shako enclosed by the black waterproof cover. The coat or 'Kollet' was dark blue, bearing the regimental distinctive colours on the collar, cuffs and shoulder-straps; cuff-flaps were dark blue. On

Regiment	Dolman and Pelisse	Facings	Lace
3rd (Brandenburg) Regiment	Dark blue	Scarlet	White
4th (1st Silesian) Regiment	Brown	Yellow	Yellow
5th (Pommeranian) Regiment	Dark blue	Dark blue	Yellow
6th (2nd Silesian) Regiment	Green	Scarlet	Yellow
8th (1st Westphalian) Regiment	Dark blue	Light blue	White
9th (Rhenish) Regiment	Light blue	Light blue	Yellow
10th (1st Magdeburg) Regiment	Green	Light blue	Yellow
11th (2nd Westphalian) Regiment	Green	Red	White

Leather equipment was black for all ranks; sabre-knots for the stirrup-hilted swords were likewise of black leather.

69. Prussia : Fusilier Officer, 2nd (1st Pommeranian) Regiment. Musketeer, 7th (2nd West Prussian) Regiment

This plate shows the uniform worn by the old 'Regular' regiments at Waterloo; the collar of the coat was officially closed to the top in 1813, but many pictures of the Waterloo period show the old-style open collar, exposing the black stock, still in use.

campaign, grey breeches and black gaiters were worn by the rank and file (though white breeches were authorised for use in summer), and overalls by the officers. Greatcoats were grey and, like the Kollet, had brass buttons.

Equipment consisted of a hide knapsack, on to which was strapped a mess-tin with white or black cover, with the greatcoat worn rolled over the shoulder. Leather equipment was white for Musketeers and black for Fusiliers; the black cartridge-pouch was worn on the hip by Musketeers, and on the front of a waist-belt by Fusiliers; the pouches of Musketeers bore oval brass plates. Short sabres were carried by Musketeers, and straight-bladed swords by Fusiliers; sword-knots were coloured to indicate the company; the all-white knot indicated the first company of the 1st Battalion of a regiment.

Officers' Kollets had longer tails, and had epaulettes with metal 'crescents', though it is possible that the older-style shoulder-straps may have been worn by some regiments. The regulation silver and black sash, and swords (curved for Fusiliers, straight-bladed for Musketeers) were a further indication of their rank. Officers, like the other ranks, often carried small packs. Their overalls had red stripes down the outer seams. Drummers were distinguished by laced 'swallow's nest' wings in the facing colour. Musket-slings were of a reddish-brown leather; bayonet-scabbards were generally discarded, the bayonets being carried fixed to the muskets. N.C.O.s had gold or silver lace on their collars and cuffs, and black and white sword-knots.

The distinctive colours of the old 'Regular' regiments present in the Waterloo campaign were as follows:

70. Prussia : Private, 1st Battalion, 12th Regiment. Private, 25th Regiment

The old Reserve infantry regiments were taken into the line in March 1815, being numbered 13 to 24; the various independent Legions and 'Freikorps' which had formed part of the Prussian Army were also taken into the line, being numbered 25 to 31. The 12th Regiment, though not officially a Reserve corps, was raised only in 1813 and was uniformed in a similar manner to the Reserve regiments.

When first raised in 1813, there was insufficient material available to clothe and equip the Reserve infantry in the regulation uniform, so a simple costume was designed, consisting of a cap, tailless jacket or sleeved waistcoat, and trousers, together with whatever equipment could be found or captured. By the middle of 1813, some regiments had received clothing from England, supplied to help Prussia to continue the war; these uniforms were either of British style, or were like those manufactured in Britain for the Portuguese Army at that time engaged in the Peninsular War. The Reserve Infantry may possibly have adopted more regulation styles by the time of Waterloo,

Regiment	Collar and Cuffs	Shoulder-straps
2nd (1st Pommeranian) Regiment	White	White
6th (1st West Prussian) Regiment	Crimson	White
7th (2nd West Prussian) Regiment	Crimson	Scarlet
9th (Colberg) Regiment	White	Scarlet
10th (1st Silesian) Regiment	Lemon Yellow	White
11th (2nd Silesian) Regiment	Lemon Yellow	Scarlet

but a large number were still wearing the unusual costumes depicted in Plates 70, 71 and 74.

The 1st Battalion of the 12th (Brandenburg) Regiment wore either the regulation Prussian shako, covered with a 'waterproof', or a grey 'Schirmütze' with a red band (in all cases, uniforms varied greatly even within individual battalions). The battalion wore black or dark grey sleeved waistcoats with red collar-patches, with white trousers; some sources indicate a double-breasted grey coat. In the 2nd Battalion, some wore a uniform like that of the 1st, while others were clothed in a more regulation style, in Kollet with red collar and cuffs and white shoulder-straps; others wore a blue Kollet with scarlet shoulder-straps and blue collar, the latter having scarlet patches. The 3rd Battalion wore either light grey sleeved waistcoats with crimson collar-patches, or captured French 'habit-vestes', with white trousers and either Prussian shakos or the 'Schirmütze'. Apart from some of the 2nd Battalion, the whole Regiment wore black leather equipment.

The 25th Regiment had previously been the infantry detachment of Lützow's 'Freikorps', one of the many volunteer units which existed in the 1813–14 war. They wore a thigh-length black 'Litewka', with red piping, black trousers and black leather equipment.

The 14th (2nd Pommeranian) Regiment (not illustrated) had Prussian shakos for all battalions. The 1st Battalion wore double-breasted blue jackets with red collars, cuffs, shoulder-straps and turnbacks, English knapsacks and white cross-belts. The 2nd Battalion wore 'English' uniforms, blue with red collars, shoulder-straps and turnbacks. The 3rd Battalion had the dark blue Kollet with red facings and brass buttons, blue trousers and white shoulder-belts.

The 15th (2nd Westphalian) Regiment (not illustrated) in all probability wore the regulation infantry uniform, with brick-red collar and cuffs, and yellow shoulder-straps to the Kollet.

71. Prussia: Private 1st Battalion, 21st Regiment. Private, 3rd Battalion, 21st Regiment

The three battalions of the 21st (4th Pommeranian) Regiment wore different uniforms. The 1st Battalion had Portuguese 'stovepipe' shakos, with brass plate and white over red plume, dark blue jackets with light green facings and shoulder-rolls, dark blue breeches and black equipment. The 2nd Battalion wore a similar uniform, but with red facings and probably red shoulder-rolls. At one time this battalion had loops of white lace on the breast of the jacket, though these had probably been removed by 1815. The 3rd Battalion was dressed in British uniforms, very similar to those of the 95th Rifles, with black facings and shoulder-rolls. Knapsacks for the entire regiment were made of grey cloth, and it seems likely that N.C.O.s bore the number of the battalion on the shoulder-straps.

The three battalions of the 19th (2nd Posen) Regiment (not illustrated) wore uniforms of a basically similar pattern, consisting of a grey 'Schirmütze', grey sleeved waistcoat, and grey breeches and gaiters. The 1st Battalion wore crimson collar-patches and shoulder-straps, and had white metal buttons. The 2nd and 3rd Battalions had grey collars, cuffs and shoulder-straps, all piped with crimson, and crimson piping down the front of the breast also. Some members of these two battalions had Prussian-style shakos made of straw and covered with the usual waterproof cover, with a large black and white Prussian cockade painted on the front. Leather equipment was blackened.

The 22nd (1st Upper Silesian) Regiment (not illustrated) wore various uniforms; the 1st Battalion had the regulation shako with black cover, grey jackets with yellow collar-patches and narrow white slides on the shoulder-straps, and grey trousers. The 2nd Battalion wore uniforms of a similar design, though the jackets were coloured blue. The 3rd Battalion also wore the same pattern of jacket, but of a grey so dark as to appear almost black. All three battalions wore black leather equipment.

The 23rd (2nd Upper Silesian) Regiment (not illustrated) wore a uniform of light grey jacket with yellow collar-patches and red shoulder-straps, and Prussian shakos. All three battalions wore the same dress.

The entire 24th (4th Brandenburg) Regiment (not illustrated) was dressed in a grey uniform with red shoulder-straps and yellow collar-patches, with shakos of the standard pattern.

The 26th (1st Magdeburg) Regiment (not illustrated) was originally known as the Elbe Regiment, being taken into the line in 1815. They wore the standard infantry uniform, the Kollet having red collar and turnbacks, bright blue cuffs with red piping, and dark blue cuff-flaps.

The 27th Regiment (not illustrated) was formed from detachments of the Elbe Regiment, dressed either in simple grey jackets or in English-manufactured costume, and from the infantry of the Hellwigsche Streifkorps, who wore Prussian shakos with a white metal hunting horn badge and black and white pompom on the front, with dark green English 'rifle' jackets, with black facings and shoulder-rolls, white piping to the facings, white metal buttons, and black leather equipment.

72/73. Prussia: Officer, 1st Uhlans.
Trooper, 6th Uhlans (ex-Lützow's Friekorps).
Trooper, 7th Uhlans (ex-Hellwig's Streifkorps).
Trooper, 6th Uhlans (ex-Bremen Volunteers).
Trooper, 7th Uhlans (ex-Von Schill's Hussars)

The three original regiments of Uhlans (Lancers) wore dark blue Kollets with red collar, cuffs and piping, with brass buttons. The regiments were distinguished by the shoulder-straps, which were white for the 1st (West Prussian) Regiment, scarlet for the 2nd (Silesian) Regiment, and yellow for the 3rd (Brandenburg) Regiment. Officers wore fringeless epaulettes, the cloth body being coloured as the other ranks' shoulder-straps. Other ranks wore a girdle around the waist, of blue with a red stripe, while officers had the regulation black and silver sash. The standard cavalry overalls were worn by all ranks. The usual shako was worn, covered with a black 'waterproof' on campaign; grey cloth caps with red bands were also used.

Other ranks were authorised to wear dark blue 'Litewka' coats on active service, with red collars, and shoulder-straps coloured as on the Kollet; but the Litewka does not seem to have been as popular with the Uhlans as with the remainder of the cavalry. Being Uhlans, N.C.O.s and troopers carried lances, with pennons coloured white over black. These latter were authorised in March 1813 to replace the earlier coloured varieties, but there may not have been opportunity to carry these orders into effect; prior to that date, the pennons had been white over blue for the 1st Regiment, red over blue for the 2nd, and yellow over blue for the 3rd. Trumpeters wore the regulation 'swallow's nest' wings, red with gold lace; shabraques were dark blue, with rounded front and rear corners, with a double red edging, though black sheep-skins with red 'wolf's teeth' edging were also used.

The 6th Uhlans were formed from Lützow's Friekorps and the Bremen Volunteers, and retained their old uniforms. The 'Lützow' element wore shakos either with or without the waterproof cover, and thigh-length Litewka-style coats, of black with red piping and shoulder-scales. Overalls and all leather equipment, including the large gauntlets, were black. The lance carried by these troops had regimental pennons of black over red. Some members of the detachment carried captured French sabretaches, of black leather and still bearing the old brass badges of the Imperial eagle. An alternative to the shako was an all-black cloth cap.

The old Bremen Volunteers, also part of the 6th Uhlans, also wore black Litewkas with red piping, but with black shoulder-straps and red collars. They were distinguished by black czapkas, which had white piping and cords, and a white pompom which bore a red cross. Their lance-pennons were red over white. All ranks of the 6th Uhlans wore black pouch-belts with brass fittings.

The 7th Uhlans were formed from the cavalry of the Hellwigsche Streifkorps and the Schill Friekorps. The Hellwig detachment wore English uniforms, of red dolmans with blue facings and white braid, together with either dark blue czapkas (as illustrated) or brown fur busbies with blue bags and white cords; some wore red pelisses with black fur trimming and white braid, and 'barrelled' sashes of red and yellow. Lance-pennons were either blue over red, or red over yellow.

The Schill Friekorps detachment wore the uniform illustrated, being a Hussar-style dress consisting of black busby and dark blue pelisse with yellow braid. The knee-patches worn on the overalls were most unusual, but the accuracy of the source of this illustration cannot seriously be doubted, being taken from an 'eye-witness' sketch.

74. Prussia: Private, 2nd Battalion, 18th Regiment. Private, 31st Regiment

The 1st Battalion of the 18th (1st Posen) Regiment wore grey coats cut in the style of a French 'surtout', with crimson collar-patches and turnback-piping, with brass buttons. Some wore Prussian shakos, but others retained the grey 'Schirmütze' with crimson band. The 2nd Battalion wore grey-sleeved waist-coats with white shoulder-straps, yellow cuffs and collar-patches, and white metal buttons. Their 'Schirmütze' was worn with a black waterproof cover, and their grey greatcoats had yellow collars. The 3rd Battalion wore dark blue-sleeved waistcoats with crimson collar-patches, dark blue caps with crimson bands, dark blue breeches, and black cross-belts. On their march from Wavre to link up with the Anglo-Allied army, this battalion is reputed to have torn off their collars in order to make marching more comfortable; to com-

memorate this, the regiment was later allowed to wear pink collars.

The 31st Regiment was originally the 2nd Infantry Brigade of the Russo-German Legion and as a result wore Russian uniforms. The shako was the characteristically-Russian scuttle-shaped 'kiwer', fitted with Prussian pompoms. The green Russian jacket had blue collar, with red cuffs, shoulder-straps, turnbacks and piping. The Russian one-piece gaiter-trousers were white for summer and grey for winter; leather equipment (including musket-slings) was black.

75. Prussia: Officer: Silesian 'Schützen' Battalion. Private, Volunteer Jäger Company, 7th Regiment

The Silesian 'Schützen' Battalion, a corps of light infantry or skirmishers, wore an infantry-style uniform in the distinctive dark green colour, with black facings and red piping. The rank and file wore black leather equipment.

In addition to the above, there existed volunteer companies of 'Frie-willigen Jäger', or riflemen, which were attached to some of the regular infantry (and cavalry) formations; the following infantry regiments, for example, had volunteer Jäger companies in the Waterloo campaign: 2nd, 6th, 9th, 10th, 11th, 12th, 14th, 15th, 24th, 25th, 27th and 28th. Generally speaking, the volunteer Jäger companies wore dark green jackets, with the facing colours of the regiment to which they were attached; the Jäger illustrated, therefore, being attached to the 7th Regiment, wore the crimson collar and cuffs and scarlet shoulder-straps which indicate that corps. Equipment was usually of the same pattern as that of the infantry, but of black leather, and sometimes brass powder-flasks were worn attached to the front of the cross-belts. More unusual were the brass-hilted sword-bayonets carried by many units. Normal infantry shakos were worn by most, though some (for example the Silesian Volunteer Jäger companies attached to the 10th and 11th Regiments) wore cloth caps, in that case with yellow bands and piping. However, there were exceptions to the general rules: Jägers of the 2nd Regiment had red piping to their white facings, and those of the 9th Regiment had cloth caps with red bands and piping, their grey overalls having a double red stripe down the outer seams.

Jäger squadrons attached to cavalry regiments usually wore the uniform of their regiment, but with a green coat bearing the regimental facings; volunteer Jägers of Hussar regiments, however, did not wear the dolman and pelisse, but, like many other cavalry Jägers, had green Litewkas. In some cases, Jäger companies were also attached to Landwehr units.

76. Prussia: Officer, Westphalian Landwehr Cavalry.

Trooper, Elbe Landwehr Cavalry.
77. Prussia: Trooper, Neumark Landwehr Cavalry.
Trooper, 3rd Silesian Landwehr Cavalry

The Landwehr, or militia, Cavalry units were, like their infantry counterparts, at first very poorly equipped, though by the time of Waterloo the worst deficiencies had been overcome and in many ways the Landwehr were almost as well armed and uniformed as the regular cavalry, though in a variety of styles, brought about by the general shortage of materials; as in the case of the old Reserve infantry, it was not uncommon to find slightly differing styles worn within the same unit.

The most common style in use at this time was the 'Litewka', though Kollets were worn by many of the rank and file as well as by officers. The shako was the most common form of head-dress, sometimes worn without the waterproof cover, though the 'Schirmütze' was not uncommon, often given an extra few inches of height by means of wire stiffeners. One feature worn by many units on their head-dress was the white cross, symbolic of the Landwehr; it was even painted on the covers of some of the shakos. The Litewka was generally dark blue, though grey and sky-blue were not unknown. The Kollet was officially authorised for use by the Landwehr in March 1815, but most continued to wear the Litewka long after this regulation, though some units had adopted the Kollet as early as 1814. Both bore regimental facing colours; overalls were almost exclusively grey, though a few were off-white. Shabraques were in Dragoon style, of dark blue with bands of the facing colour, but the black sheepskin was more popular. Lance-pennons were officially black and white, though many bore the Landwehr cross, and numbers were in the 'provincial' colours. It should be explained here that in the Prussian Army, each province was assigned a distinctive facing colour, worn by all the regiments of that area, with coloured shoulder-straps the way of identifying individual regiments from a province; though of course there were many exceptions to this basic rule. Officers' uniforms usually consisted of a Kollet, with regimental distinctions like those of the other ranks, grey overalls, and the universal silver and black sash.

Of the regiments present in the Waterloo campaign, the following various uniform distinctions were worn:

The 1st Kurmark Landwehr Cavalry are shown wearing French-style 'stovepipe' shakos, with a band of white lace around the top, and a Prussian cockade in front (white with a black centre). Red collar and shoulder-straps; blue cuffs piped red. The same regiment is shown in another illustration with red cuffs and shoulder-straps and a blue collar to the Kollet.

In addition to the uniform illustrated (Plate 76), Westphalian Landwehr Cavalry are shown wearing blue collar and cuffs to the Litewka, piped bright green. Some Westphalians wore the Kollet instead of the Litewka from 1814. Lance-pennons are shown in some sources as blue over black, green over white, and red over orange with a black cross thereon. White cords and caplines were worn on some Westphalian shakos. With the Kollet was worn a dark blue girdle, edged bright green (other ranks only).

The facing colour of the Elbe regiments was light blue, though some wore dark blue Litewkas with dark blue facings; some of their shakos had a rear peak, and bore a white cross and Prussian pompom on the front. White sheepskin shabraques were used by some; lance-pennons were blue over red.

The Neumark regiments were equipped in English uniforms, wearing 'stovepipe' shakos with white lace, white crosses, and cords of mixed red and white. The grey shabraques with red heart-shaped decorations were quite unique to these regiments. Lance-pennons were white over black.

The Pommeranian facing colour was white; some of the Pommeranians wore grey Litewkas instead of the regulation blue.

The 3rd Silesian Landwehr Cavalry wore dark blue Uhlan-style czapkas as illustrated. The facing colour of the Silesian regiments was yellow. The 2nd Silesian are shown with dark blue Kollets with yellow collar and cuffs, red shoulder-straps, dark blue overalls with black strapping, and red and yellow

Hussar-style 'barrelled' sashes. Some Silesians had white sheepskin shabraques with yellow edging. Cloaks were white with yellow collar and lining. Lance-pennons were white over yellow for the 1st Regiment, yellow over white for the 2nd, and yellow over red for the 3rd, though yellow over blue and blue over yellow were also known. The volunteer Jäger squadrons of the Silesian regiments had dark green Litewkas with yellow collars and piping, dark green overalls, and their lance-pennons were variously recorded as blue over yellow, brown over yellow, or with a green triangle nearest to the top of the shaft, with two crimson or red 'tails'.

It should be remembered that the details given above are taken mainly from contemporary illustrations, and may only be the dress of part of any specific regiment; in all probability, a number of different uniforms were worn in each regiment at the same time.

78. Prussia: Private, 1st Pommeranian Landwehr. Officer, 1st Elbe Landwehr

When first mobilised, the militia or Landwehr of the Prussian Army were without doubt the most wretchedly-equipped body in Europe, often dressed in rags, with no shoes, and poor weapons. By 1815, however, almost all the deficiencies had been made up, and the Landwehr infantry was as well clothed and armed as many of the regular corps.

The head-dress was the cloth 'Schirmütze', of dark blue or black, with piping and bands of the facing colour, with the white 'Landwehr cross' and the black and white Prussian cockade on the front. The caps on occasion had black waterproof covers. The Litewka varied in length from thigh to knee-length, was of dark blue or black (blue being by far the most common in 1815), with coloured facings. The facing and button-colours of those provinces whose Landwehr were engaged in the Waterloo campaign are given below:

Province	Facings	Buttons
Westphalia	Green	White
Elbe	Light blue	Yellow
Pommerania	White	Yellow
Silesia	Yellow	White

The shoulder-straps of the Litewka often indicated the number of the regiment within each province, as in the regular infantry, viz. 1st Regiment, white; 2nd, scarlet; 3rd, yellow; 4th, light blue. By this method (which was not universal), for example, the 1st Silesian Landwehr had yellow facings (provincial colour) and white shoulder-straps (seniority colour). Although officers could wear the Litewka, many wore the standard infantry Kollet with regimental facings. By 1815 many regiments had their number embroidered on their shoulder-straps. Legwear consisted of loose white, grey or sometimes blue trousers, or white or grey breeches worn with black gaiters. Officers' rank was indicated in the usual way, but N.C.O.s had thin white braids around their collars and cuffs. Most N.C.O.s and drummers carried short sabres; drummers had red and white 'swallow's nest' wings. Equipment varied from the standard infantry pattern to just one haversack or cartridge-pouch, or a rolled blanket over one shoulder. Some still carried the large axes with which the early Landwehr regiments had been armed. Bayonet-scabbards were never carried, those Landwehr corps possessing bayonets keeping them permanently fixed.

79. Prussia : Gunner, Foot Artillery. N.C.O., Horse Artillery

Artillery uniforms of the Prussian Army followed the style of infantry and cavalry; the Foot Artillery wore dark blue infantry Kollets, with black collars and cuffs, red piping and red turnbacks. Horse Artillery wore cavalry pattern Kollets in the same colourings, except that the turnbacks were dark blue, trimmed with a black braid which had red edges. Shoulder-straps were red for both. The Horse Artillery, in field dress, also wore the Litewka, with collar and shoulder-straps as on the Kollet, but with plain cuffs. Legwear was styled according to the infantry or cavalry patterns. Shakos were invariably covered with black 'waterproofs' on campaign.

Foot Artillerymen were equipped and armed as infantry, gunners carrying muskets and N.C.O.s short carbines;

belts were black leather, and cartridge-pouches bore brass badges of a three-flamed grenade. Horse Artillerymen carried cavalry sabres; their leather-work was white. The two artillerymen illustrated in this plate show the closed version of the collar, officially introduced in 1813, though some may have worn the old 'open-necked' version.

Officers' rank was distinguished in the usual way; their greatcoats were grey for the Foot branch and blue for the Horse, both with black velvet collars and red piping. Artillery shabraques were dark blue, Dragoon-style, edged with red, those of the officers having an edging of five thin red lines.

The following were the batteries present during the Waterloo campaign:

Foot batteries, 12-lb. cannon – Nos. 2, 3, 4, 5, 6, 7, 8, 9 and 13.
Foot batteries, 6-lb. cannon – Nos. 1, 2, 3, 5, 7, 8, 10, 11, 12, 13, 14, 15, 18, 21, 34, 35 and 37.
Howitzer battery No. 1.
Horse batteries Nos. 1, 2, 5, 6, 7, 10, 11, 12, 14, 18, 19 and 20.

giving a total of 312 guns. Of the above, the 13th and 21st 6-lb. Foot batteries, and the 12th Horse battery, were Landwehr units. Traditionally, the carriages of Prussian ordnance were painted light blue.

The 20th Horse battery wore a special uniform, being the costume of the old Berg Horse Artillery, consisting of the shako with brass crossed cannons badge and chin-scales, red pompom and cords, and a light blue cockade with white centre below the pompom. Dark blue double-breasted jacket, with red collar, cuffs and turnbacks; dark blue shoulder-straps piped red. Brass buttons. Dark blue breeches, worn with black Hessian boots which were ornamented with red lace and tassels; black leather pouch-belt and an all-steel stirrup-hilted sabre carried on a white waist-belt with a brass plate completed the uniform. Officers were distinguished in the normal way.

80. Prussia: Driver, Train. Krankenträger (Stretcher-bearer)

The 'Train' of the Prussian Army was responsible for the transport of all equipment, drove regimental transport, and generally carried out all routine duties. The uniform consisted of a shako with black and white pompom and rosette, and a simple jacket known as a 'Trainjacke', of dark blue with light blue collar and red shoulder-straps. Mounted detachments wore cavalry overalls, but dismounted men wore grey breeches and black gaiters; those mounted carried a cavalry sabre on a black waist-belt, while those on foot were armed with a carbine, and had a cartridge-pouch on a black leather shoulder-belt. The 'Truppentrain', the detachments attached to drive regimental transport, wore the facings of the unit to which they were seconded.

Medical officers were attached to all units; they wore infantry-style uniforms with dark blue facings piped red, and gilt buttons. The shako was the regulation head-dress, but various types of cap were adopted by some medical officers, especially those attached to Landwehr units. The surgeons were assisted by 'Krankenträger' or stretcher-bearers, who wore grey caps, Litewkas and breeches, with dark blue facings and black gaiters. They were armed with short sabres.

Medical facilities were crude in the extreme; although each army had a complement of trained medical officers, they were hopelessly inadequate in strength to cope with the vast number of casualties with which they had to contend. The techniques of field surgery, performed at great speed in insanitary conditions, were so rudimentary that the simplest wound might result in death. Chances of survival after an operation or amputation were extremely thin: perhaps one in three had the luck to survive.

BLACK AND WHITE ILLUSTRATIONS

FIG. 1. Showing the area of the campaign, with troop dispositions at 0900 hrs., 18 June 1815.

FIG. 2. Showing the battle of Waterloo, with troop dispositions at 1100 hrs., 18 June 1815.

FIG. 3. BRITISH FLAGS. King's Colour, 1st Foot Guards (top); Regimental Colour, 5th Line Battalion, King's German Legion (bottom).

British and German Legion infantry units each carried two flags or Colours, one consisting basically of the Union Flag, or 'King's Colour', and one bearing regimental devices, or 'Regimental Colour'; this nomenclature was reversed in the regiments of Foot Guards, the Union being the Regimental Colour. Each battalion of Foot Guards possessed three King's Colours, these being called the Colonel's, Lieutenant-Colonel's and Major's, each bearing distinguishing features; the 1st Guards carried the Major's Colour at Waterloo. The field was crimson, with a small Union in the upper canton, from which issued a gold 'pile wavy', the distinguishing feature of the Major's Colour. The other devices consisted of a Crown in 'proper' (i.e. natural) colours, a gold reversed 'G.R.' cipher, and two honour-scrolls bearing the words 'Corunna' and 'Lincelles'. The Foot Guards possessed a large number of Regimental Colours, one per company, each bearing the device of that company. The Regimental Colour carried by the 1st Guards at Waterloo consisted of the Union, with the gold numerals 'VIII' in the upper canton nearest the pole, with the central device of the red dragon of Wales, with a Crown above, the badge of the eighth company, with the honour-scrolls as on the Major's Colour. The pike-heads were, like all those of the British infantry, gilt and spear-shaped; two crimson and gold cords hung from the top of the pole, each with a large tassel.

The German Legion Regimental Colours were all similar, being in the dark blue facing colour, with the Small Union, the central device being a wreath in 'proper' colours, with a smaller wreath and lettering in gold, the only difference between battalions being the number in the title, for example 'King's German Legion V Battalion'. The 'Peninsula' honour was borne in gold letters above the wreath. King's Colours consisted of the Union, with the central devices as on the Regimental Colours.

FIG. 4. BRITISH FLAGS. King's Colour, 14th Foot (top); Regimental Colour, 33rd Foot (bottom).

The King's Colour of the 14th consisted of the Union, with a central device of a red shield, edged yellow, bearing 'XIV REGT.' in gold letters, the whole surrounded by a wreath in 'proper' colours. The Regimental Col-

Fig 3. British flags

Fig 4. British flags

our, like all those of the British Infantry, had a field of the regimental facing colour, in this case light buff, with the same central device as on the King's Colour, and the usual small Union.

The Regimental Colour of the 33rd consisted of the standard of St. George (a white field with a large red cross), with the small Union, and a central device consisting of a red shield bearing 'XXXIII REGT.' in gold letters, surrounded by a wreath. This was the one Regimental Colour which did not have a field in the regimental facing colour. The King's Colour was the Union Flag, with the central device as on the Regimental Colour.

British Colours were all 6 feet by 6 feet 6 inches; no cavalry standards were carried in the Waterloo campaign.

FIG. 5. BRUNSWICK FLAGS. 2nd Line Battalion (*top*); 3rd Line Battalion (*bottom*).

The Colours of the Brunswick Line Battalions (the Light did not carry flags) varied greatly in design; the two illustrated are examples. That of the 2nd Battalion consisted of a light blue field with a black horizontal stripe, bearing the crowned cipher 'F.W.', within a wreath, all in gold. The pike-heads were either the letters 'F.W.' with a crown above, or the white horse in a similar-shaped surround, made in gilt. Cords were either silver and yellow or gold and light blue. The 3rd Line Battalion carried a colour with a light blue centre and black surround, bearing a white

horse and the motto 'NUNQUAM RETRORSUM' in black letters.

FIG. 6. NASSAU AND PRUSSIAN FLAGS. 2nd Nassau Regiment (*top*); 1st Battalion, 10th Prussian Regiment (*bottom*).

The standard carried by the 2nd Nassau Regiment had a golden-yellow field, bearing a light blue inner, surrounded by a green wreath. On the inner patch was a golden rampant lion, with gold 'piles' or vertical bars.

In the Waterloo campaign, only one standard was carried by each of the two Musketeer battalions per Prussian infantry regiment. The 10th and 11th regiments carried standards of this pattern. Those of the 10th Regiment (the same for both battalions) had a deep rose field, with a white central patch bearing a black eagle. The scroll above the eagle, bearing the motto 'Pro Gloria et Patria', was also deep rose. All embroidery, including the laurel wreath, was gold.

The standards of the 11th Regiment, also alike for both battalions, had sky-blue fields, with white centres bearing the black eagle, sky-blue scrolls and silver embroidery.

FIG. 7. PRUSSIAN FLAGS. 1st Battalion, 2nd Regiment (*top*); 2nd Battalion, 9th Regiment (*bottom*).

The 1st Battalion of the 2nd Regiment had a standard with a white field, bearing a black 'wavy' cross, with a black centre bearing a golden eagle and white scroll. All embroidery was gold;

Fig 5. Brunswick flags

Fig 6. Nassau and Prussian flags

Fig 7. Prussian flags

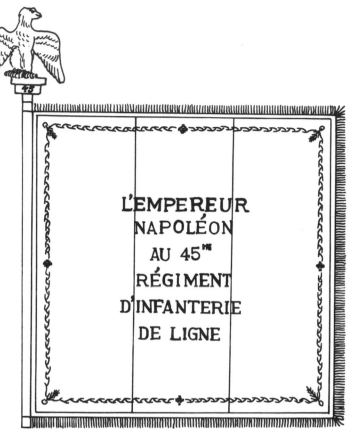

L'EMPEREUR
NAPOLÉON
AU 45ᵐᵉ
RÉGIMENT
D'INFANTERIE
DE LIGNE

AUSTERLITZ
JENA
FRIEDLAND
ESSLING
WAGRAM

Fig 8. 'Eagle', 45th French Regiment

as for all Prussian infantry standards, the pike-heads were gilt, bearing the 'F.W.R.' cipher, from which hung silver and black streamers and tassels. The 2nd Battalion of the 2nd Regiment had a standard of a black field with white centre and wavy cross, black eagle and scroll, and gold embroidery. The 6th Regiment also carried standards of a similar pattern, that of the 1st Battalion having a white field, red cross, white centre bearing a black eagle and red scroll, and silver embroidery; the 2nd Battalion had a green field with red cross, white centre with black eagle and green scroll, and silver embroidery.

The 2nd Battalion of the 9th Regiment had a standard which consisted of a large black 'Iron Cross' on a white field, with an orange centre bearing a black eagle and sky-blue scroll, and gold embroidery. The 1st Battalion of the 9th Regiment had a similar standard, but with a white cross on a black field. Both battalions bore the battle honour 'Colberg 1807' in gold letters on a sky-blue oval.

The 7th Regiment had standards of the 'Iron Cross' design, but with 'flying' eagles. That of the 1st Battalion had a white cross on a lemon field, a lemon centre with red scroll and black eagle, and silver embroidery; that of the 2nd Battalion was the same, but with the cross and scroll of sky-blue.

Flag-poles of the 9th, 10th and 11th Regiments were black, and white for the remainder.

Landwehr and the ex-Reserve regiments officially did not carry flags, though many were used unofficially, a plain black flag with large white cross being most popular, though the Silesian Landwehr favoured sky-blue flags bearing yellow Silesian eagles

FIG. 8. 'EAGLE', 45th French Regiment.

The 1815 pattern of flag carried by the French Army consisted of the 'tricolor' of red, white and blue vertical bands, the blue being nearest the flag-pole, the white in the middle, and the red on the outside. Gone was the elaborate embroidery of former days, the flags being ornamented with only a thin line of gold embroidery, with a gold fringe around the outside. The inscription on one side, in gold letters, was similar for all regiments: 'L'Empereur Napoléon Au —— Régiment D'Infanterie De Ligne', the regimental number being the only distinguishing feature. On the reverse side of the flag were the regimental battle-honours, those of the 45th being 'Austerlitz', 'Jena', 'Friedland', 'Essling' and 'Wagram'. The flag of the 105th Regiment, captured by the 'Union' Brigade like that of the 45th, bore the honours 'Jena', 'Eylau', 'Eckmuhl', 'Essling' and 'Wagram'. Above the flag was the gilded 'Eagle', the real regimental symbol. The flag-poles were dark blue, and below the head hung 'tricolor' streamers with gold embroidery.

APPENDIX

Order of Battle — The Anglo-Allied Army

1st CORPS (THE PRINCE OF ORANGE)

1st Division (Maj.-Gen. Cooke)

  1st British Brigade (Maj.-Gen. Maitland)

    1st and 3rd Btns., 1st Foot Guards

  2nd British Brigade (Maj.-Gen. Sir J. Byng)

    2nd Btn., 2nd Foot Guards; 2nd Btn., 3rd Foot Guards

  Artillery (Lt.-Col. Adye)

    Captain Sandham's Battery, Royal Foot Artillery; Major Kuhlmann's Battery, King's German Legion Horse Artillery

3rd Division (Lt.-Gen. Sir Charles Alten)

  5th British Brigade (Maj.-Gen. Sir C. Halkett)

    2nd Btn., 30th Regt.; 33rd Regt.; 2nd Btn., 69th Regt.; 2nd Btn., 73rd Regt.

  2nd King's German Legion Brigade (Col. von Ompteda)

    1st and 2nd Light Btns.; 5th and 8th Line Btns.

  1st Hanoverian Brigade (Maj.-Gen. Count Kielmannsegge)

    Field-Btns. Bremen, Verden and York; Light Btns. Lüneburg and Grubenhagen; Field-Jäger Corps

  Artillery (Lt.-Col. Williamson)

    Major Lloyd's Battery, Royal Foot Artillery; Captain Cleeves's Battery, King's German Legion Foot Artillery

2nd Netherlands Division (Lt.-Gen. Baron de Perponcher)

  1st Brigade (Maj.-Gen. Count Bylandt)

    7th Infantry; 27th Jägers; 5th, 7th and 8th Militia

  2nd Brigade (Prince Bernhard of Saxe-Weimar)

    2nd Nassau Regiment; Regiment of Orange Nassau

  Artillery (Major van Opstal)

    Captain Byleveld's Battery, Horse Artillery; Captain Stievenaar's Battery, Foot Artillery

3rd Netherlands Division (Lt.-Gen. Baron Chassé)

  1st Brigade (Maj.-Gen. Ditmers)

    2nd Infantry; 35th Jägers; 4th, 6th, 17th and 19th Militia

  2nd Brigade (Maj.-Gen. d'Aubremé)

    3rd, 12th and 13th Infantry; 36th Jägers; 3rd and 10th Militia

Artillery (Major van der Smissen)
> Captain Krahmer's Battery, Horse Artillery; Captain Lux's Battery, Foot Artillery

2nd CORPS (LT.-GEN. LORD HILL)

2nd Division (Lt.-Gen. Sir H. Clinton)

3rd British Brigade (Maj.-Gen. Adam)
> 1st Btn., 52nd Light Infantry; 1st Btn., 71st Light Infantry; 2nd and 3rd Btns., 95th Rifles

1st King's German Legion Brigade (Col. du Plat)
> 1st, 2nd, 3rd and 4th Line Btns.

3rd Hanoverian Brigade (Col. H. Halkett)
> Landwehr Btns. Bremervörde, Osnabrück, Quackenbrück and Salzgitter

Artillery (Lt.-Col. Gold)
> Captain Bolton's Battery, Royal Artillery; Major Sympher's Battery, King's German Legion Horse Artillery

4th Division (Lt.-Gen. Sir Charles Colville)

4th British Brigade (Col. Mitchell)
> 3rd Btn., 14th Regt.; 1st Btn., 23rd Fusiliers; 51st Light Infantry

6th British Brigade (Maj.-Gen. Johnstone)
> 2nd Btn., 35th Regt.; 1st Btn., 54th Regt.; 2nd Btn., 59th Regt.; 1st Btn., 91st Regt.

6th Hanoverian Brigade (Maj.-Gen. Sir J. Lyon)
> Field-Btns. Lauenberg and Calenburg; Landwehr Btns. Nienburg, Hoya and Bentheim

Artillery (Lt.-Col. Hawker)
> Major Brome's Battery, Royal Foot Artillery; Captain von Rettburg's Battery, Hanoverian Foot Artillery

1st Netherlands Division (Lt.-Gen. Stedmann)

1st Brigade (Maj.-Gen. Hauw)
> 4th and 6th Infantry; 16th Jägers; 9th, 14th and 15th Militia

2nd Brigade (Maj.-Gen. Eerens)
> 1st Infantry; 18th Jägers; 1st, 2nd and 18th Militia

Artillery
> Captain Wynand's Battery, Foot Artillery

Netherlands Indian Brigade (Lt.-Gen. Anthing)
> 5th Infantry; Battalion of Flanquers; 10th and 11th Jägers; Captain Riesz's Battery, Foot Artillery

Appendix

RESERVE

5th Division (Lt.-Gen. Sir T. Picton)

  8th British Brigade (Maj.-Gen. Sir J. Kempt)

   1st Btn., 28th Regt.; 1st Btn., 32nd Regt.; 1st Btn., 79th Highlanders; 1st Btn., 95th Rifles

  9th British Brigade (Maj.-Gen. Sir D. Pack)

   3rd Btn., 1st Regt.; 1st Btn., 42nd Highlanders; 2nd Btn., 44th Regt.; 1st Btn., 92nd Highlanders

  5th Hanoverian Brigade (Col. von Vincke)

   Landwehr Btns. Hameln, Gifhorn, Peine and Hildesheim

  Artillery (Major Heisse)

   Major Roger's Battery, Royal Foot Artillery; Captain Braun's Battery, Hanoverian Foot Artillery

6th Division (Lt.-Gen. Hon. Sir L. Cole)

  10th British Brigade (Maj.-Gen. Sir J. Lambert)

   1st Btn., 4th Regt.; 1st Btn., 27th Regt.; 1st Btn., 40th Regt.; 2nd Btn., 81st Regt.

  4th Hanoverian Brigade (Col. Best)

   Landwehr Btns. Lüneburg, Verden, Osterode and Münden

  Artillery (Lt.-Col. Brückmann)

   Major Unett's Battery, Royal Foot Artillery; Captain Sinclair's Battery, Royal Foot Artillery

British Reserve Artillery (Major Drummond)

  Lt.-Col. Ross's Battery, R.H.A.; Major Beane's Battery, R.H.A.; Major Morrisson's Battery, R.F.A.; Captain Hutchesson's Battery, R.F.A.; Captain Ibert's Battery, R.F.A.

7th Division

  7th British Brigade

   2nd Btn., 25th Regt.; 2nd Btn., 37th Regt.; 2nd Btn., 78th Regt.

British Garrison Troops

  13th Veteran Btn.; 2nd Garrison Btn.; 1st Foreign Btn.

The Brunswick Corps (Duke of Brunswick)

  Advanced Guard Btn. (Major von Rauschenplatt)

  Light Brigade (Lt.-Col. von Buttlar)

   Guard Btn.; 1st, 2nd and 3rd Light Btns.

  Line Brigade (Lt.-Col. von Specht)

   1st, 2nd and 3rd Line Btns.

  Artillery (Major Mahn)

   Captain Heinemann's Battery, Horse Artillery; Major Moll's Battery, Foot Artillery

Hanoverian Reserve Corps (Lt.-Gen. von der Decken)
  1st Brigade (Lt.-Col. von Bennigsen)
    Field-Btn. Hoya; Landwehr Btns. Mölln and Bremerlehe
  2nd Brigade (Lt.-Col. von Beaulieu)
    Landwehr Btns. Nordheim, Ahlefeldt and Springe
  3rd Brigade (Lt.-Col. Bodecker)
    Landwehr Btns. Otterndorf, Zelle and Ratzeburg
  4th Brigade (Lt.-Col. Wissel)
    Landwehr Btns. Hanover, Uelzen, Neustadt and Diepholz
Nassau Contingent (General von Kruse)
  1st Infantry

CAVALRY
  1st British Brigade (Maj.-Gen. Lord Somerset)
    1st and 2nd Life Guards; Royal Horse Guards; 1st Dragoon Guards
  2nd British Brigade (Maj.-Gen. Sir W. Ponsonby)
    1st, 2nd and 6th Dragoons
  3rd British Brigade (Maj.-Gen. Sir W. Dörnberg)
    23rd Light Dragoons; 1st and 2nd Light Dragoons, King's German Legion
  4th British Brigade (Maj.-Gen. Sir J. Vandeleur)
    11th, 12th and 16th Light Dragoons
  5th British Brigade (Maj.-Gen. Sir C. Grant)
    7th and 15th Hussars; 2nd Hussars, King's German Legion
  6th British Brigade (Maj.-Gen. Sir H. Vivian)
    10th and 18th Hussars; 1st Hussars, King's German Legion
  7th British Brigade (Col. Sir F. von Arentsschildt)
    13th Light Dragoons; 3rd Hussars, King's German Legion
  British Horse Artillery (attached to Cavalry)
    Major Bull's Battery, R.H.A.; Lt.-Col. Webber Smith's Battery, R.H.A.;
      Lt.-Col. Sir R. Gardiner's Battery, R.H.A.; Captain Whinyates' Battery
      (Mounted Rocket Corps), R.H.A.; Captain Mercer's Battery, R.H.A.;
      Captain Ramsay's Battery, R.H.A.
  1st Hanoverian Brigade (Col. von Estorff)
    Prince Regent's Hussars; Bremen and Verden Hussars; Duke of Cumberland's
      Hussars
  Cavalry of the Brunswick Corps
    Regt. of Hussars; Regt. of Uhlans
  1st Netherlands Brigade (Maj.-Gen. Trip)
    1st and 3rd Dutch Carabiniers; 2nd Belgian Carabiniers

2nd Netherlands Brigade (Maj.-Gen. de Ghigny)
  4th Dutch Light Dragoons; 8th Belgian Hussars
3rd Netherlands Brigade (Maj.-Gen. van Merlen)
  5th Belgian Light Dragoons; 6th Dutch Hussars
Netherlands Horse Artillery (attached to Cavalry)
  Captain Petter's half-battery; Captain Gey's half-battery
Engineers, etc.
  Corps of Royal Engineers (British); Corps of Royal Sappers and Miners (British);
    Royal Waggon Train (British); Royal Staff Corps (British)

TOTAL STRENGTH ANGLO-ALLIED ARMY
  Infantry   82,062
  Cavalry   14,482
  Artillery   8,166
  Engineers, etc.   1,240
    Total   105,950 men and 204 guns

Order of Battle — The French Army

IMPERIAL GUARD (LT.-GEN. COUNT DROUOT)
  Lt.-Gen. Count Friant
    1st and 2nd Grenadiers
  Lt.-Gen. Count Roguet
    3rd and 4th Grenadiers
  Lt.-Gen. Count Morand
    1st and 2nd Chasseurs
  Lt.-Gen. Count Michel
    3rd and 4th Chasseurs
  Lt.-Gen. Count Duhesme
    1st and 3rd Tirailleurs
  Lt.-Gen. Count Barrois
    1st and 3rd Voltigeurs
  Lt.-Gen. Lefebvre-Desnöettes
    Lancers and Chasseurs à Cheval
  Lt.-Gen. Count Guyot
    Dragoons, Grenadiers à Cheval and Gendarmerie d'Elite
  Lt.-Gen. Desvaux de St. Maurice
    9 Batteries, Guard Foot Artillery; 4 Batteries, Guard Horse Artillery;
      Marines of the Guard; Engineers of the Guard

1st ARMY CORPS (LT.-GEN. COUNT D'ERLON)
1st Division (Lt.-Gen. Allix)
  1st Brigade (Brig.-Gen. Quiot)
    54th and 55th Light Infantry
  2nd Brigade (Brig.-Gen. Bourgeois)
    28th and 105th Infantry
2nd Division (Lt.-Gen. Baron Donzelot)
  1st Brigade (Brig.-Gen. Schmitz)
    13th Light Infantry, 17th Infantry
  2nd Brigade (Brig.-Gen. Baron Aulard)
    19th and 31st Infantry
3rd Division (Lt.-Gen. Baron Marcognet)
  1st Brigade (Brig.-Gen. Noguès)
    21st and 46th Infantry
  2nd Brigade (Brig.-Gen. Grenier)
    25th and 45th Infantry
4th Division (Lt.-Gen. Count Durutte)
  1st Brigade (Brig.-Gen. Pegot)
    8th and 29th Infantry
  2nd Brigade (Brig.-Gen. Brue)
    85th and 95th Infantry
1st Cavalry Division (Lt.-Gen. Baron Jaquinot)
  1st Brigade (Brig.-Gen. Bruno)
    7th Hussars and 3rd Chasseurs à Cheval
  2nd Brigade (Brig.-Gen. Baron Gobrecht)
    3rd and 4th Lancers
Artillery
  5 Batteries, Foot Artillery; 1 Battery, Horse Artillery; Engineers

2nd ARMY CORPS (LT.-GEN. COUNT REILLE)
5th Division (Lt.-Gen. Baron Bachelu)
  1st Brigade (Brig.-Gen. Baron Husson)
    2nd Light Infantry, 61st Infantry
  2nd Brigade (Brig.-Gen. Baron Campi)
    72nd and 108th Infantry
6th Division (Lt.-Gen. Prince Jerome Napoleon)
  1st Brigade (Brig.-Gen. Baron Baudouin)
    1st Light Infantry and 3rd Infantry
  2nd Brigade (Brig.-Gen. Soye)
    1st and 2nd Infantry

7th Division (Lt.-Gen. Count Girard)
  1st Brigade (Brig.-Gen. de Villiers)
    11th Light Infantry, 82nd Infantry
  2nd Brigade (Brig.-Gen. Baron Piat)
    12th Light Infantry, 4th Infantry
9th Division (Lt.-Gen. Count Foy)
  1st Brigade (Brig-Gen. Baron Gauthier)
    92nd and 93rd Infantry
  2nd Brigade (Brig.-Gen. Jamin)
    4th Light Infantry, 100th Infantry
2nd Cavalry Division (Lt.-Gen. Baron Piré)
  1st Brigade (Brig.-Gen. Baron Hubert)
    1st and 6th Chasseurs à Cheval
  2nd Brigade (Brig.-Gen. Baron Wathiez)
    5th and 6th Lancers
Artillery
  5 Batteries, Foot Artillery; 1 Battery, Horse Artillery; Engineers

3rd ARMY CORPS (LT.-GEN. COUNT VANDAMME)
8th Division (Lt.-Gen. Baron Lefol)
  1st Brigade (Brig.-Gen. Baron Billiard)
    15th Light Infantry, 23rd Infantry
  2nd Brigade (Brig.-Gen. Baron Corsin)
    37th and 64th Infantry
10th Division (Lt.-Gen. Baron Habert)
  1st Brigade (Brig.-Gen. Gengoult)
    34th and 88th Infantry
  2nd Brigade (Brig.-Gen. Dupeyroux)
    22nd and 70th Infantry, 2nd Swiss Regt.
11th Division (Lt.-Gen. Baron Berthezène)
  1st Brigade (Brig.-Gen. Dufour)
    12th and 56th Infantry
  2nd Brigade (Brig.-Gen. Baron Lagarde)
    33rd and 86th Infantry
3rd Cavalry Division (Lt.-Gen. Baron Domon)
  1st Brigade (Brig.-Gen. Baron Dommanget)
    4th and 9th Chasseurs à Cheval
  2nd Brigade (Brig.-Gen. Baron Vinot)
    12th Chasseurs à Cheval

Artillery
    4 Batteries, Foot Artillery; 1 Battery, Horse Artillery; Engineers

4th ARMY CORPS (LT.-GEN. COUNT GÉRARD)
12th Division (Lt.-Gen. Count Pêcheux)
  1st Brigade (Brig.-Gen. Rome)
    30th and 96th Infantry
  2nd Brigade (Brig.-Gen. Baron Shoeffer)
    6th Light Infantry, 63rd Infantry
13th Division (Lt.-Gen. Baron Vichery)
  1st Brigade (Brig.-Gen. Baron le Capitaine)
    59th and 76th Infantry
  2nd Brigade (Brig.-Gen. Desprez)
    48th and 69th Infantry
14th Division (Lt.-Gen. de Bourmont) (deserted, and replaced by Hulot)
  1st Brigade (Brig.-Gen. Hulot)
    9th Light Infantry, 111th Infantry
  2nd Brigade (Brig.-Gen. Toussaint)
    44th and 50th Infantry
7th Cavalry Division (Lt.-Gen. Baron Maurin)
  1st Brigade (Brig.-Gen. Baron Vallin)
    6th Hussars, 8th Chasseurs à Cheval
  2nd Brigade (Brig.-Gen. Berruyer)
    6th, 11th and 16th Dragoons (also 15th Dragoons, detached to 9th Cavalry
      Division by 10 June)
Artillery
    4 Batteries, Foot Artillery; 1 Battery, Horse Artillery; Engineers

6th ARMY CORPS (LT.-GEN. COUNT LOBAU)
19th Division (Lt.-Gen. Baron Simmer)
  1st Brigade (Brig.-Gen. Baron de Bellair)
    5th and 11th Infantry
  2nd Brigade (Brig.-Gen. Jamin)
    27th and 84th Infantry
20th Division (Lt.-Gen. Baron Jeanin)
  1st Brigade (Brig.-Gen. Bony)
    5th Light Infantry, 10th Infantry
  2nd Brigade (Brig.-Gen. de Tromelin)
    47th and 107th Infantry (47th detached to La Vendée)

Appendix

21st Division (Lt.-Gen. Baron Teste)
  1st Brigade (Brig.-Gen. Baron Lafitte)
    8th Light Infantry, 40th Infantry (40th organising at Senlis)
  2nd Brigade (Brig.-Gen. Baron Penne)
    65th and 75th Infantry
Artillery
  4 Batteries, Foot Artillery; 1 Battery, Horse Artillery; Engineers

1st CAVALRY CORPS (LT.-GEN. COUNT PAJOL)
4th Cavalry Division (Lt.-Gen. Baron Soult)
  1st Brigade (Brig.-Gen. St. Laurent)
    1st and 4th Hussars
  2nd Brigade (Brig.-Gen. Ameil)
    5th Hussars
5th Cavalry Division (Lt.-Gen. Baron Subervie)
  1st Brigade (Brig.-Gen. de Colbert)
    1st and 2nd Lancers
  2nd Brigade (Brig.-Gen. Merlin de Douai)
    11th Chasseurs à Cheval
Artillery
  2 Batteries, Horse Artillery

2nd CAVALRY CORPS (LT.-GEN. COUNT EXELMANS)
9th Cavalry Division (Lt.-Gen. Baron Strolz)
  1st Brigade (Brig.-Gen. Baron Burthe)
    5th and 13th Dragoons
  2nd Brigade (Brig.-Gen. Baron Vincent)
    15th and 20th Dragoons
10th Cavalry Division (Lt.-Gen. Baron Chastel)
  1st Brigade (Brig.-Gen. Baron Bennemains)
    4th and 12th Dragoons
  2nd Brigade (Brig.-Gen. Berton)
    14th and 17th Dragoons
Artillery
  2 Batteries, Horse Artillery

3rd CAVALRY CORPS (LT.-GEN. KELLERMANN)
11th Cavalry Division (Lt.-Gen. Baron L'Héritier)
  1st Brigade (Brig.-Gen. Baron Picquet)
    2nd and 7th Dragoons
  2nd Brigade (Brig.-Gen. Baron Guiton)
    8th and 11th Cuirassiers

12th Cavalry Division (Lt.-Gen. Roussel d'Hurbal)
  1st Brigade (Brig.-Gen. Baron Blanchard)
    1st and 2nd Carabiniers
  2nd Brigade (Brig.-Gen. Donop)
    2nd and 3rd Cuirassiers
Artillery
  2 Batteries, Horse Artillery

4th CAVALRY CORPS (LT.-GEN. COUNT MILHAUD)
13th Cavalry Division (Lt.-Gen. Wathier)
  1st Brigade (Brig.-Gen. Baron Dubois)
    1st and 4th Cuirassiers
  2nd Brigade (Brig.-Gen. Travers)
    7th and 12th Cuirassiers
14th Cavalry Division (Lt.-Gen. Baron Delort)
  1st Brigade (Brig.-Gen. Baron Vial)
    5th and 10th Cuirassiers
  2nd Brigade (Brig.-Gen. Baron Farine)
    6th and 9th Cuirassiers
Artillery
  Two Batteries, Horse Artillery

TOTAL STRENGTH, FRENCH ARMY
  Infantry   83,758
  Cavalry   20,959
  Artillery   10,028
  Engineers, etc.   1,384
    Total   116,129 men and 350 guns

Order of Battle — The Prussian Army

1st ARMY CORPS (LT.-GEN. VON ZIETEN)
  1st Brigade (Gen. von Steinmetz)
    12th and 24th Infantry; 1st Westphalian Landwehr; 1st and 3rd Silesian
      Jäger companies
  2nd Brigade (Gen. von Pirch II)
    6th and 28th Infantry; 2nd Westphalian Landwehr
  3rd Brigade (Gen. von Jagow)
    7th and 29th Infantry; 3rd Westphalian Landwehr; 2nd and 4th Silesian
      Jäger companies

4th Brigade (Gen. von Henkel)

19th Infantry; 4th Westphalian Landwehr

Cavalry (Lt.-Gen. von Röder)

Brigade of Gen. von Treskow

2nd and 5th Dragoons; Brandenburg Uhlans

Brigade of Lt.-Col. von Lützow

6th Uhlans; 1st and 2nd Kurmark Landwehr Cavalry; 1st Silesian Hussars; 1st Westphalian Landwehr Cavalry

Artillery (Col. von Lehmann)

Foot Artillery 12-pounder batteries Nos. 2, 6 and 9; Foot Artillery 6-pounder batteries Nos. 1, 3, 7, 8 and 15; Howitzer battery No. 1; Horse Artillery batteries Nos. 2, 7 and 10

2nd ARMY CORPS (GENERAL VON PIRCH I)

5th Brigade (Gen. von Tippelskirchen)

2nd and 25th Infantry; 5th Westphalian Landwehr

6th Brigade (Gen. von Krafft)

9th and 26th Infantry; 1st Elbe Landwehr

7th Brigade (Gen. von Brause)

14th and 22nd Infantry; 2nd Elbe Landwehr

8th Brigade (Col. von Langen)

21st and 23rd Infantry; 3rd Elbe Landwehr

Cavalry (Gen. von Jürgass)

Brigade of Col. von Thümen

Silesian Uhlans; 6th Dragoons; 11th Hussars

Brigade of Col. Count Schulenburg

1st Dragoons; 4th Kurmark Landwehr Cavalry

Brigade of Lt.-Col. von Sohr

3rd and 5th Hussars; 5th Kurmark Landwehr Cavalry; Elbe Landwehr Cavalry

Artillery (Col. von Röhl)

Foot Artillery 12-pounder batteries Nos. 4 and 8; Foot Artillery 6-pounder batteries Nos. 5, 10, 12, 34 and 37; Horse Artillery batteries Nos. 5, 6 and 14

3rd ARMY CORPS (LT.-GEN. VON THIELEMANN)

9th Brigade (Gen. von Borcke)

8th and 36th Infantry; 1st Kurmark Landwehr

10th Brigade (Col. von Kämpfen)

27th Infantry; 2nd Kurmark Landwehr

11th Brigade (Col. von Luck)
  3rd and 4th Kurmark Landwehr
12th Brigade (Col. von Stülpnagel)
  31st Infantry; 5th and 6th Kurmark Landwehr
Cavalry (Gen. von Hobe)
  Brigade of Col. von der Marwitz
    7th and 8th Uhlans; 9th Hussars
  Brigade of Col. Count Lottum
    5th Uhlans; 7th Dragoons; 3rd and 6th Kurmark Landwehr Cavalry
Artillery (Col. von Mohnhaupt)
  Foot Artillery 12-pounder battery No. 7; Foot Artillery 6-pounder battery
    Nos. 18 and 35; Horse Artillery batteries Nos. 18, 19 and 20

4th ARMY CORPS (GENERAL COUNT BÜLOW VON DENNEWITZ)
  13th Brigade (Lt.-Gen. von Hacke)
    10th Infantry; 2nd and 3rd Neumark Landwehr
  14th Brigade (Gen. von Ryssel)
    11th Infantry; 1st and 2nd Pommeranian Landwehr
  15th Brigade (Gen. von Losthin)
    18th Infantry; 3rd and 4th Silesian Landwehr
  16th Brigade (Col. von Hiller)
    15th Infantry; 1st and 2nd Silesian Landwehr
Cavalry (Gen. Prince William of Prussia)
  Brigade of Gen. von Sydow
    1st Uhlans; 2nd and 8th Hussars
  Brigade of Col. Count Schwerin
    10th Hussars; 1st and 2nd Neumark Landwehr Cavalry; 1st and 2nd
      Pommeranian Landwehr Cavalry
  Brigade of Lt.-Col. von Watzdorf
    1st, 2nd and 3rd Silesian Landwehr Cavalry
Artillery (Lt.-Col. von Bardeleben)
  Foot Artillery 12-pounder batteries Nos. 3, 5 and 13; Foot Artillery 6-
    pounder batteries Nos. 2, 11, 13, 14 and 21; Horse Artillery batteries
    Nos. 1, 11 and 12

TOTAL STRENGTH, PRUSSIAN ARMY
  Infantry   99,715
  Cavalry   11,879
  Artillery etc.   5,303
    Total   116,897 men and 350 guns

Strengths of the Opposing Armies

With strengths varying from day to day, and with existing records often conflicting, the following tables can only be regarded as approximate.

ANGLO-ALLIED ARMY

1st Corps	1st Division	4,061
	3rd Division	6,970
	2nd Netherlands Division	7,533
	3rd Netherlands Division	6,669
	Total: 1st Corps 25,233 men and 56 guns	
2nd Corps	2nd Division	6,833
	4th Division	7,212
	1st Netherlands Division	6,389
	Netherlands Indian Brigade	3,583
	Detachments from 6th and 7th Btns., K.G.L.	14
	Orderlies	2
	Total: 2nd Corps 24,033 men and 40 guns	
Reserve	5th Division	7,158
	6th Division	5,149
	7th Division and Garrison Troops	3,233
	Brunswick Corps	5,376
	Hanoverian Reserve Corps	9,000
	Nassau Contingent	2,880
	Total: Reserve 32,796 men and 64 guns	
Cavalry	(44 British RHA guns attached)	14,482
Artillery		8,166
Engineers, etc.		1,240

FRENCH ARMY

Imperial Guard	Infantry	12,554
	Cavalry	3,590
	Artillery	3,175 and 96 guns
	Engineers	109
1st Army Corps	Infantry	16,200
	Cavalry	1,400
	Artillery	1,066 and 46 guns
	Engineers	330

2nd Army Corps	Infantry	19,750
	Cavalry	1,729
	Artillery	1,385 and 46 guns
	Engineers	409
3rd Army Corps	Infantry	14,058
	Cavalry	932
	Artillery	936 and 38 guns
	Engineers	146
4th Army Corps	Infantry	12,589
	Cavalry	2,366
	Artillery	1,538 and 38 guns
	Engineers	201
6th Army Corps	Infantry	8,152
	Artillery	743 and 38 guns
	Engineers	189
1st Cavalry Corps	Cavalry	2,324
	Artillery	317 and 12 guns
2nd Cavalry Corps	Cavalry	2,817
	Artillery	246 and 12 guns
3rd Cavalry Corps	Cavalry	3,245
	Artillery	309 and 12 guns
4th Cavalry Corps	Cavalry	2,556
	Artillery	313 and 12 guns

PRUSSIAN ARMY

1st Army Corps	Infantry	27,817
	Cavalry	1,925
	Artillery	1,019 and 96 guns
2nd Army Corps	Infantry	25,836
	Cavalry	4,468
	Artillery	1,454 and 80 guns
3rd Army Corps	Infantry	20,611
	Cavalry	2,405
	Artillery	964 and 48 guns
4th Army Corps	Infantry	25,381
	Cavalry	3,081
	Artillery	1,866 and 88 guns

BIBLIOGRAPHY

The literature relating to the Hundred Days campaign of 1815 is vast. The following bibliography is in no way comprehensive, but includes many of the most important works. Those listed are primarily English-language editions; details of reprints of original editions are noted mainly in those cases which include revisions or a new introduction. A useful bibliography and commentary on sources is 'the Hundred Days: A Political and Military perspective' by D. P. Resnick and G. de Bertier de Sauvigny, in *Napoleonic Military History: A Bibliography*, ed. D. D. Horward, London 1986. Part I of the following bibliography is concerned primarily with the history of the campaign, some of the significant memoirs, regimental histories which concentrate on the campaign, and works of more general relevance; Part II is concerned primarily with armies and uniforms.

I

Batty, R. *An Historical Sketch of the Campaign of 1815*, London 1820.

Becke, A. F. *Napoleon and Waterloo: The Emperor's Campaign with the Armée du Nord, 1815, A Strategical and Tactical Study*, London 1914, revised 1939, r/p London 1995.

Boulger, D. C. *The Belgians at Waterloo*, London 1901.

Brett-James, A. *The Hundred Days*, London 1964 (collection of first-hand accounts).

Caldwell, G., & Cooper, R. *Rifle Green at Waterloo*, 1990 (95th Rifles in the Waterloo campaign, including nominal rolls).

Chandler, D. G. *The Campaigns of Napoleon*, London 1967.

Chandler, D. G. *Dictionary of the Napoleonic Wars*, London 1979.

Chandler, D. G. *Waterloo: The Hundred Days*, London 1980.

Clark-Kennedy, A. E. *Attack the Colour! The Royal Dragoons in the Peninsula and at Waterloo*, London 1975.

Costello, E. *The Adventures of a Soldier, or, Memoirs of Edward Costello*, London 1847; originally published in *United Service Journal*, r/p as *The Peninsular and Waterloo Campaigns: Edward Costello*, ed. A. Brett-James, London 1967.

Cotton, E. *A Voice from Waterloo*, 1849; 9th rev. edn., Brussels 1900.

Dalton, C. *The Waterloo Roll Call*, London 1904.

De Lancey, Lady M. *A Week at Waterloo in 1815*, ed. B. R. Ward, London 1906.

Esposito, Brig. Gen. V. J., & Elting, Col. J. R. *A Military History and Atlas of the Napoleonic Wars*, London 1964.

Fortescue, Hon. Sir John *History of the British Army*, Vol. X, London 1920; the section on Waterloo was reprinted as *The Campaign of Waterloo*, London 1987.

Fraser, Sir William Bt. *Words on Wellington*, London 1889.

Gore, Capt. A. *An Historical Account of the Battle of Waterloo ... intended to explain and elucidate the Topographical Plan executed by W. B. Craan ...*, Brussels 1817.

Gourgaud, G. *The Campaign of MDCCCXV*, London 1818.

Griffiths, A. *Wellington and Waterloo*, London 1898.

Hamilton-Williams, D. C. *Waterloo New Perspectives: The Great Battle Reappraised*, London 1993.

Haythornthwaite, P. J. *The Napoleonic Source*

Book, London 1990.

Hibbert, C. (ed.) *The Wheatley Diary*, London 1964.

Holme, N., & Kirby, E. L. *Medal Rolls, 23rd Foot, Royal Welch Fusiliers, Napoleonic Period*, Caernarfon & London 1978.

Houssaye, H. *1815: Waterloo*, trans. A. E. Mann, ed. A. Euan-Smith, London 1900.

Howarth, D. *A Near Run Thing*, London 1968.

Jackson, Lt. Col. B. *Notes and Reminiscences of a Staff Officer chiefly relating to the Waterloo Campaign*, ed. R. C. Seaton, London 1903.

Jones, G. *The Battle of Waterloo*, London 1852.

Kelly, C. *The Memorable Battle of Waterloo*, London 1817.

Kennedy, Sir James Shaw *Notes on the Battle of Waterloo*, London 1865 (the author, who served at Waterloo, was known as James Shaw until his marriage in 1820).

Kincaid, Sir John *Adventures in the Rifle Brigade*, London 1830; r/p in Maclaren's combined edn., London 1908, with *Random Shots from a Rifleman*, London 1835.

Knollys, Major *Shaw The Life Guardsman*, London 1885.

Lachouque, H. *Waterloo 1815*, Paris 1972.

Lachouque, H., & Brown, A. S. K. *The Anatomy of Glory*, London 1962 (history of Napoleon's Imperial Guard).

Lagden, A., & Sly, J. *The 2/73rd at Waterloo*, Brightlingsea 1988.

Lawrence, W. *The Autobiography of Sergeant William Lawrence*, ed. G. N. Bsnkes, London 1886.

Leeke, Revd. W. *History of Lord Seaton's Regiment (the 52nd Light Infantry) at The Battle of Waterloo*, London 1866; and supplement to the same, London 1871.

Low, E. B. *With Napoleon at Waterloo*, ed. McK. MacBride, London 1911.

Mann, M. *And They Rode On: The King's Dragoon Guards at Waterloo*, Salisbury 1984.

Maxwell, Sir Herbert *The Life of Wellington*, London 1900.

Mercer, Gen. A. C. *Journal of the Waterloo Campaign*, Edinburgh & London 1870.

Morris, T. *Recollections of Military Service in 1813, 1814, and 1815*, London 1845; r/p as *The Napoleonic Wars: Thomas Morris*, ed. J. Selby, London 1967.

Müffling, F. C. F. von *History of the Campaign of 1815*, ed. Sir John Sinclair Bt., London 1816; r/p with intro. by Maj. Gen. B. P. Hughes, Wakefield 1970.

Naylor, J. *Waterloo*, London 1960.

'Near Observer' *The Battle of Waterloo*, London 1816.

Nofi, A. *The Waterloo Campaign*, London 1993.

Paget, J., & Saunders, D. *Hougoumont: The Key to Victory at Waterloo*, London 1992.

Pattison, F. H. *Personal Recollections of the Waterloo Campaign*, Glasgow 1873.

Ropes, J. C. *The Campaign of Waterloo: A Military History*, New York 1892.

Saunders, E. *The Hundred Days*, London 1964.

Siborne, Maj. Gen. H. T. (ed.) *The Waterloo Letters*, London 1891.

Siborne, W. *History of the War in France and Belgium in 1815*, London 1844; r/p entitled *History of the Waterloo Campaign*, London 1990.

Simmons, G. *A British Rifle Man*, ed. W. Verner, London 1899.

Tomkinson, W. *The Diary of a Cavalry Officer in the Peninsula and Waterloo Campaign*, ed. J. Tomkinson, London 1895.

Uffindell, A. *The Eagle's Last Triumph: Napoleon's Victory at Ligny, June 1815*, London 1994.

Vansittart, J. *Surgeon James's Journal*, London 1964.

Weller, J. *Wellington at Waterloo*, London 1967.

Wellington, Duke of *Dispatches of Field Marshal the Duke of Wellington*, ed. J. Gurwood, London 1834–38.

Wood, Gen. Sir Evelyn *Cavalry in the Waterloo Campaign*, London 1895.

Wootton, G. *Waterloo 1815: The Birth of Modern Europe*, London 1992.

II

Beaufort, L. de *Waterloo* (series of uniform-plates).

Bucquoy, E. L. *Les Uniformes du Premier Empire*, ed. Lt. Col. Bucquoy & G. Devautour; volumes include the following, of most relevance to Waterloo, all published in Paris: *Dragon et Guides*, 1980; *La Cavalerie Légère*, 1980; *La Garde Impériale: Troupes à Cheval*, 1977, and *Troupes à Pied*, 1977; *L'Infanterie*, 1979; *Les Cuirassiers*, 1978.

Bukhari, E. *Napoleon's Cuirassiers and Carabiniers*, London 1977.

Bukhari, E. *Napoleon's Hussars*, London 1978.

Bukhari, E. *Napoleon's Line Chasseurs*, London 1977.

Elting, Col. J. R. *Swords Around A Throne: Napoleon's Grande Armée*, London 1989 (very important modern study of the French army).

Elting, Col. J. R., & Knötel, H. *Napoleonic Uniforms*, New York 1993.

Fletcher, I. *Wellington's Foot Guards*, London 1994.

Fosten, B. *Wellington's Heavy Cavalry*, London 1982.

Fosten B. *Wellington's Infantry, I and II*, London 1981–82.

Fosten, B. *Wellington's Light Cavalry*, London 1982.

Griffith, P. *French Artillery*, London 1976.

Haswell Miller, A. E., & Dawnay, N. P. *Military Drawings and Paintings in the Royal Collection*, London 1966–70 (reproduces a number of pictures executed at the time of Waterloo or just after).

Haythornthwaite, P. J. *British Infantry of the Napoleonic Wars*, London 1987.

Haythornthwaite, P. J. *Napoleon's Guard Infantry, I and II*, London 1984–85.

Haythornthwaite, P. J. *Napoleon's Light Infantry*, London 1983.

Haythornthwaite, P. J. *Napoleon's Line Infantry*, London 1983.

Haythornthwaite, P. J. *Napoleon's Specialist Troops*, London 1988.

Haythornthwaite, P. J. *The Armies of Wellington*, London 1994.

Haythornthwaite, P. J. *Wellington's Specialist Troops*, London 1988.

Hofschröer, P. *Prussian Cavalry of the Napoleonic Wars, II (1807–15)*, London 1986.

Hofschröer, P. *Prussian Landwehr and Landsturm*, London 1980.

Hofschröer, P. *Prussian Light Infantry 1792–1815*, London 1984.

Hofschröer, P. *Prussian Line Infantry 1792–1815*, London 1984.

Hofschröer, P. *Prussian, Reserve, Militia and Irregular Troops*, London 1987.

Hofschröer, P. *The Hanoverian Army of the Napoleonic Wars*, London 1989.

Knötel, R. *Uniformenkunde* (classic series of prints by one of the greatest uniform historians).

Knötel, R., Knötel, H., & Sieg, H. *Handbuch der Uniformkinde*, Hamburg 1937, r/p 1964; English-language edn. entitled *Uniforms of the World*, trans. R. G. Ball, London 1980.

Lawson, C. C. P. *History of the Uniforms of the British Army*, Vols. IV, V, London 1966–67.

Malibran, H. *Guide . . . des Uniformes de l'Armée française, de 1780 à 1848*, Paris 1904–07, r/p Krefeld 1972 (primarily concerned with uniforms but includes material on organisation and lineage).

Mollo, J. *Waterloo Uniforms: British Cavalry*, London 1973.

Nash, D. *The Prussian Army 1808–15*, New Malden 1972.

Norman, C. A. 'The Dutch-Belgian Army at Waterloo', in the periodical *Tradition*, issues 46–48 and 60.

Pivka, O. von *Brunswick Troops 1809–15*, London 1985 (a revision of the same author's *The Black Brunswickers*, London 1973).

Pivka, O. von *Napoleon's German Allies: Nassau and Oldenburg*, London 1976.

Reid, S. *Wellington's Highlanders*, London 1992.

Rousselot, L. *L'Armée Française (series of uniform-plates)*.

Young, P. *Blücher's Army*, London 1973.